Not For Children CHILDREN'S BOOKS

The Littlest Bitch

Published by Sellers Publishing, Inc.

161 John Roberts Road, South Portland, Maine 04106
For ordering information:
(800) 625-3386 Toll free
(207) 772-6814 Fax
Visit our Web site: www.sellerspublishing.com
E-mail: rsp@rsvp.com

Not-for-Children Children's Books™

ISBN: 13: 978-1-4162-0568-5

10 9 8 7 6 5 4 3 2 1

Printed and bound in China.

Not For Children CHILDREN'S BOOKS

The Littlest Bitch

Written by David Quinn & Michael Davis

Illustrated by Devon Devereaux

SELLERS
PUBLISHING

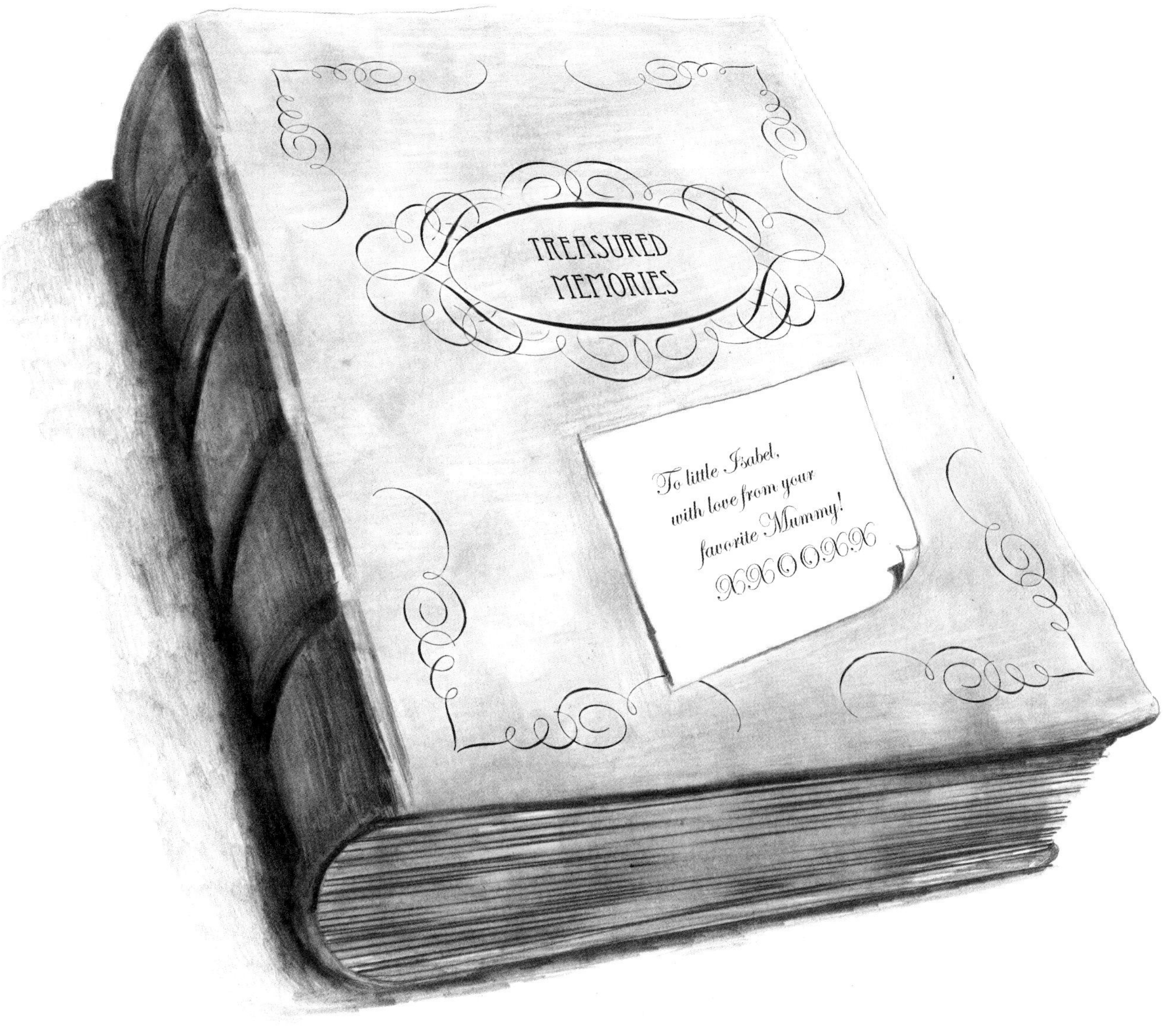
TREASURED MEMORIES
To little Isabel,
with love from your
favorite Mummy!
XXOOXX

Here's Mummy's Perfect Little Princess in her party dress. Isabel had just turned four years old when Daddy took this picture – according to her direction, of course.

So precocious – she insisted on wearing Mummy's pearls.

At least they used to be Mummy's.

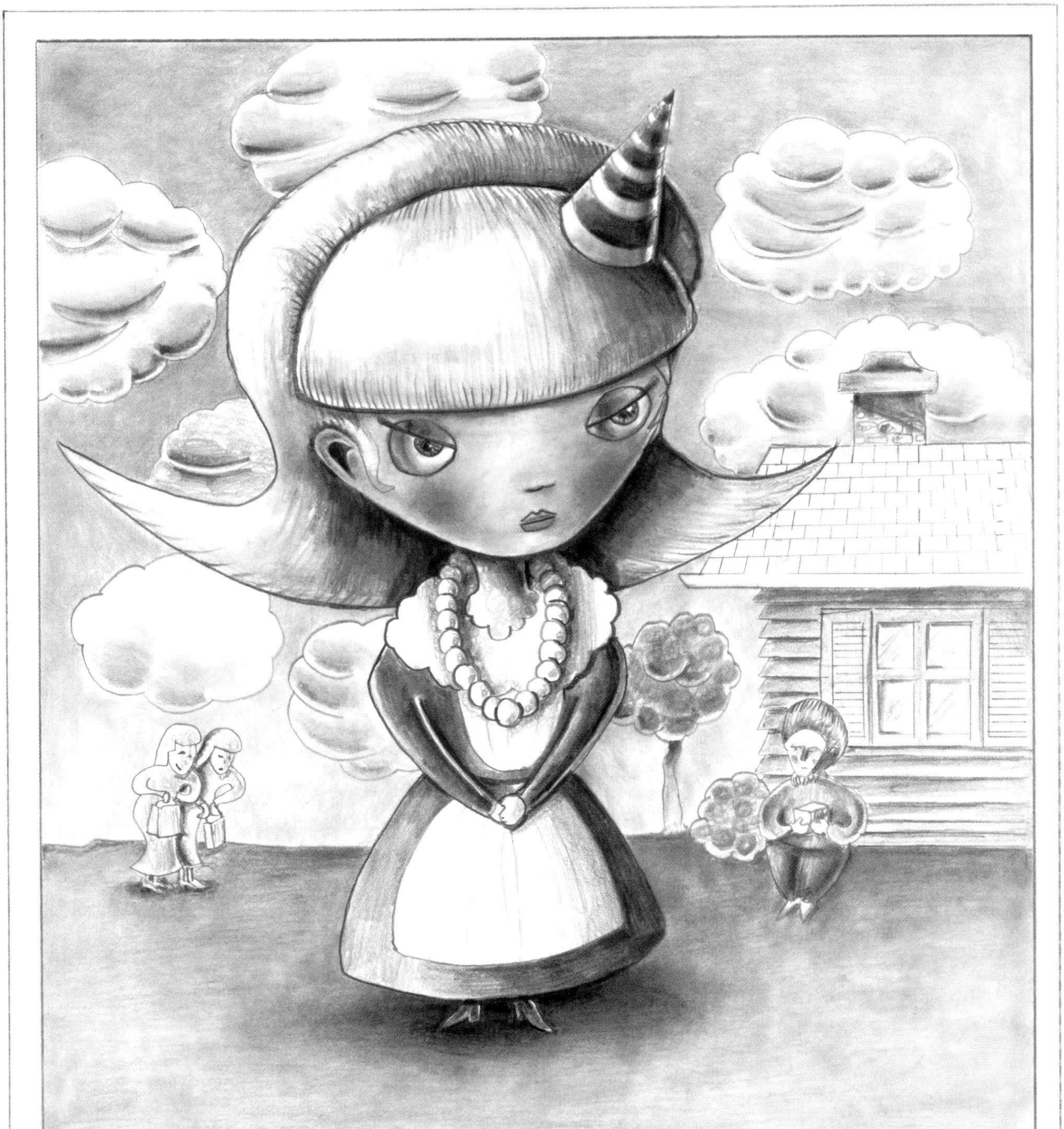

Yes, Isabel is a very, very grown-up girl.
She always says "Please," and she always says
"Thank you."

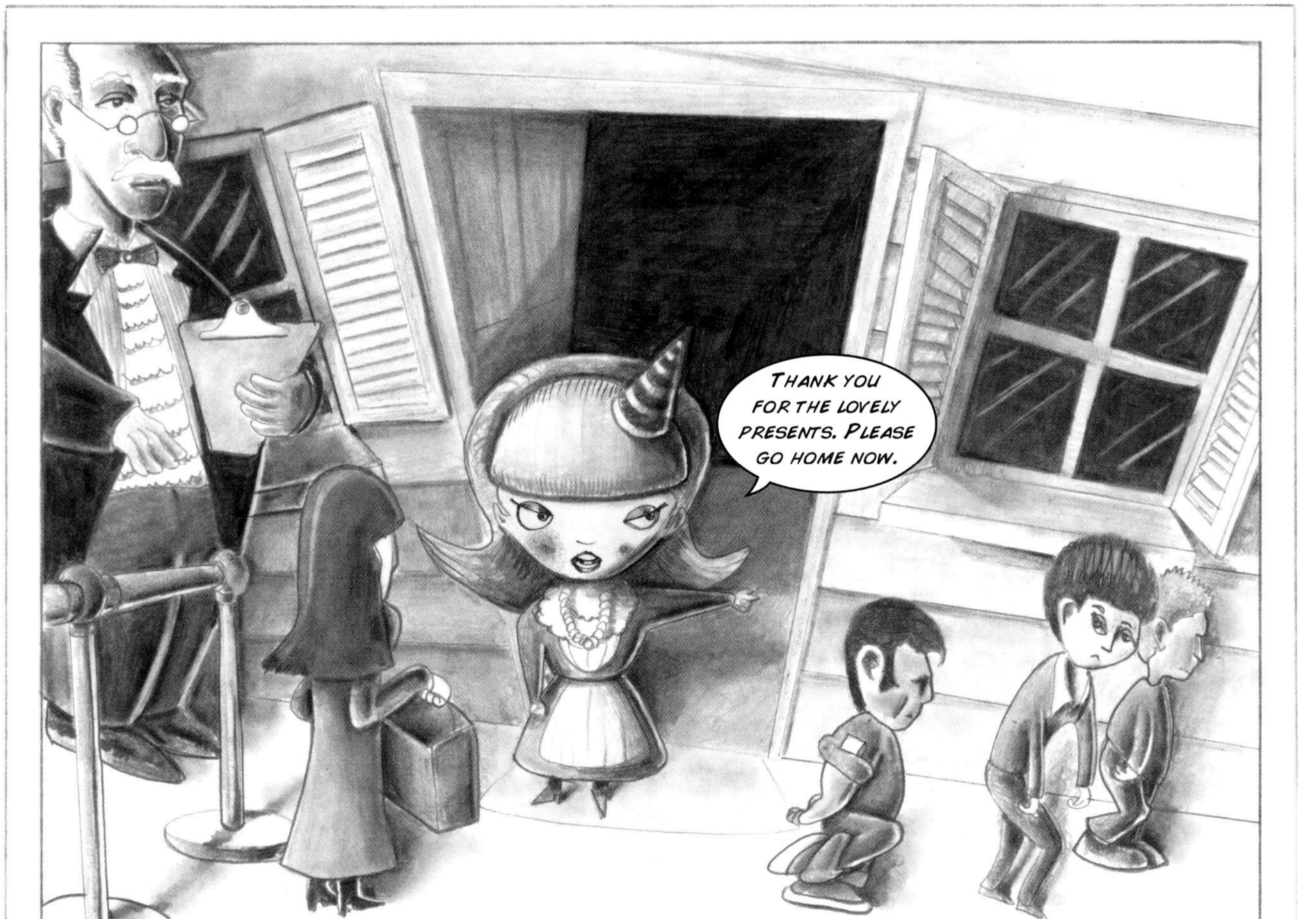
THANK YOU FOR THE LOVELY PRESENTS. PLEASE GO HOME NOW.

And when it comes to setting an example for her little sister – well, not every child has Isabel's knack for giving till it hurts.

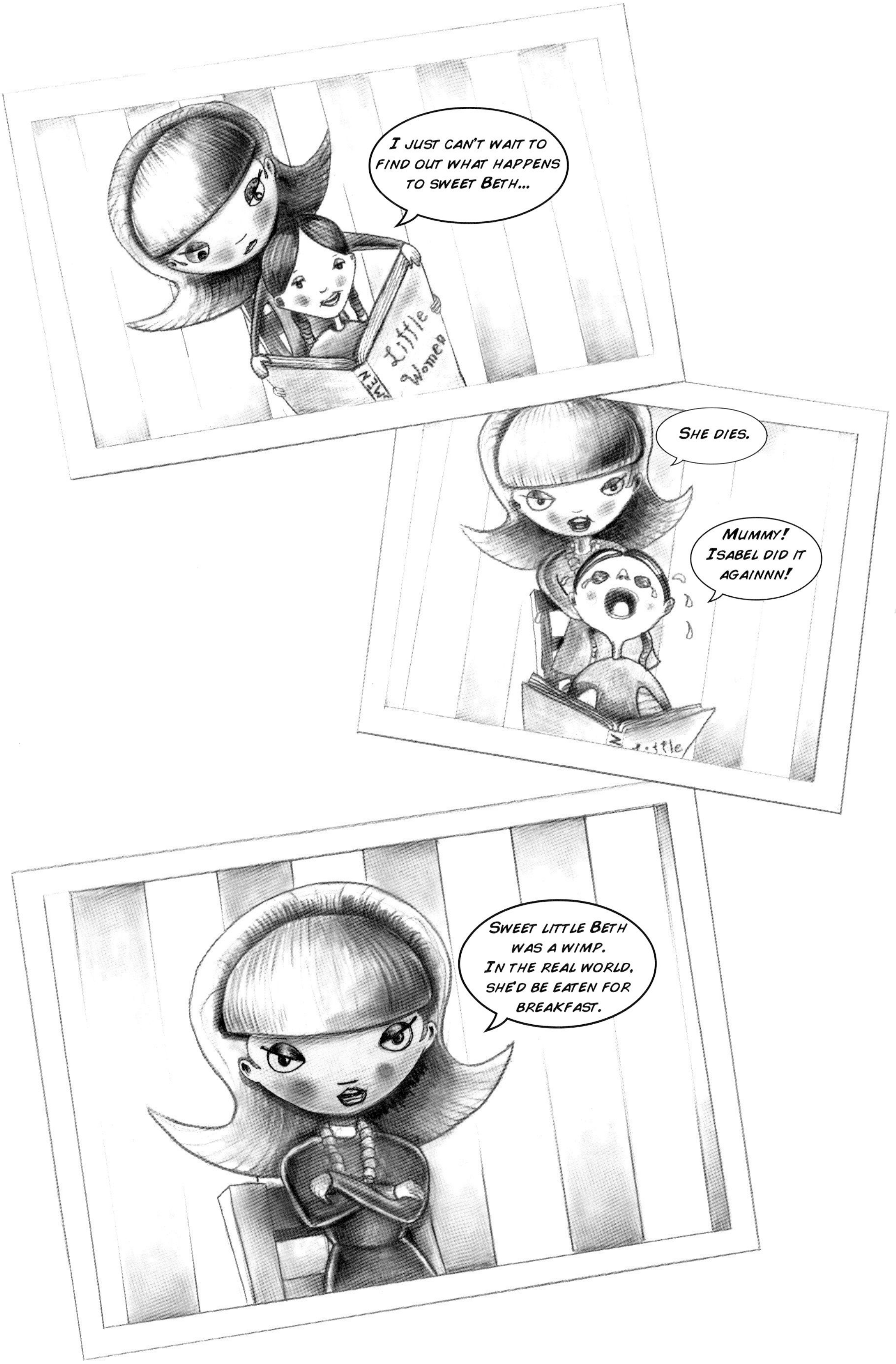
I JUST CAN'T WAIT TO FIND OUT WHAT HAPPENS TO SWEET BETH...
Little Women
SHE DIES.
MUMMY! ISABEL DID IT AGAINNN!
SWEET LITTLE BETH WAS A WIMP. IN THE REAL WORLD, SHE'D BE EATEN FOR BREAKFAST.

For her fifth birthday, Mummy's Little Darling
presented us with a gift wish list that raised
just a few eyebrows – but she kept us all
so entertained!

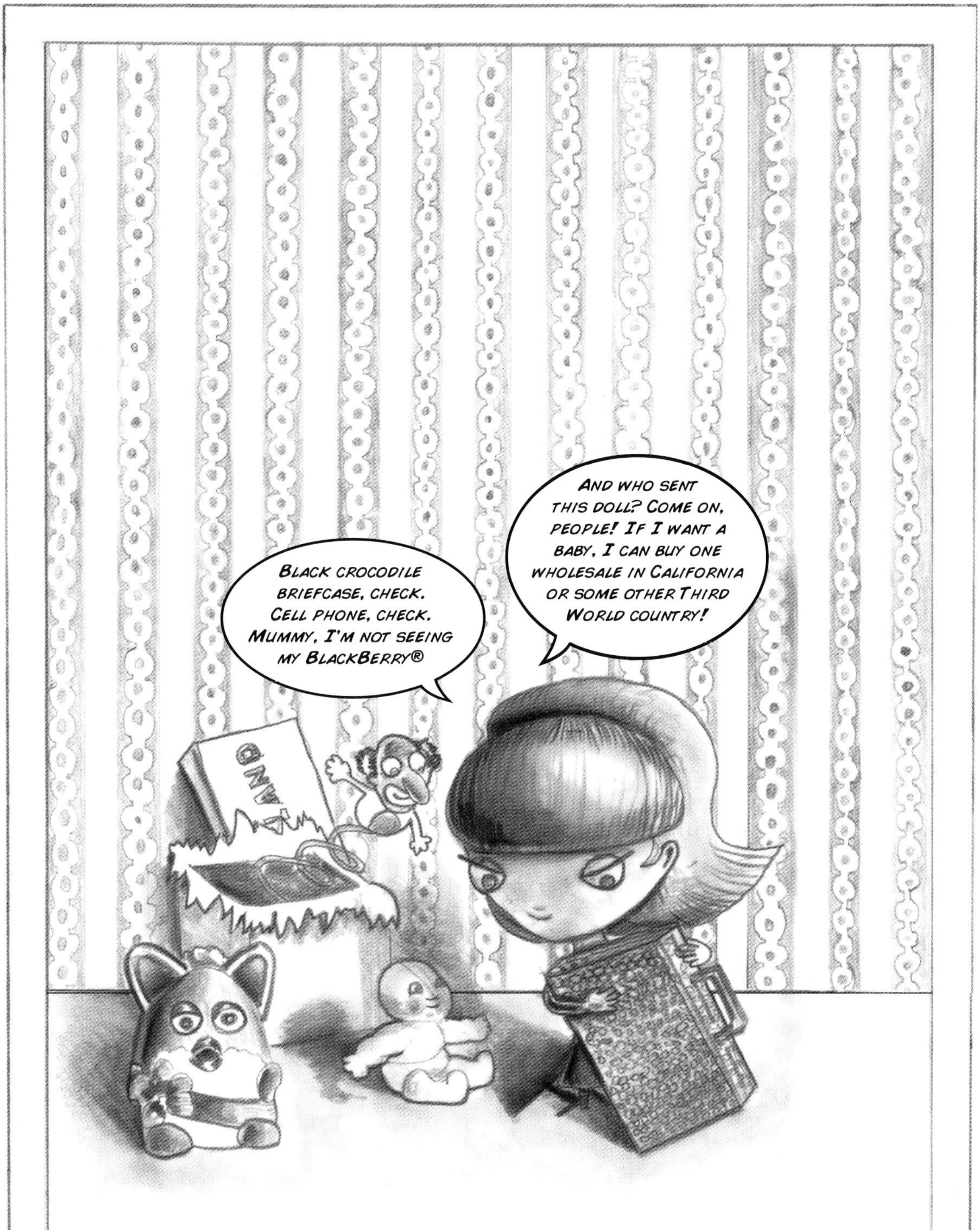
Black crocodile briefcase, check. Cell phone, check. Mummy, I'm not seeing my BlackBerry®
And who sent this doll? Come on, people! If I want a baby, I can buy one wholesale in California or some other Third World country!
AND

Here she is playing "Performance Review" with each member of the family, providing such a stimulating time for us all!

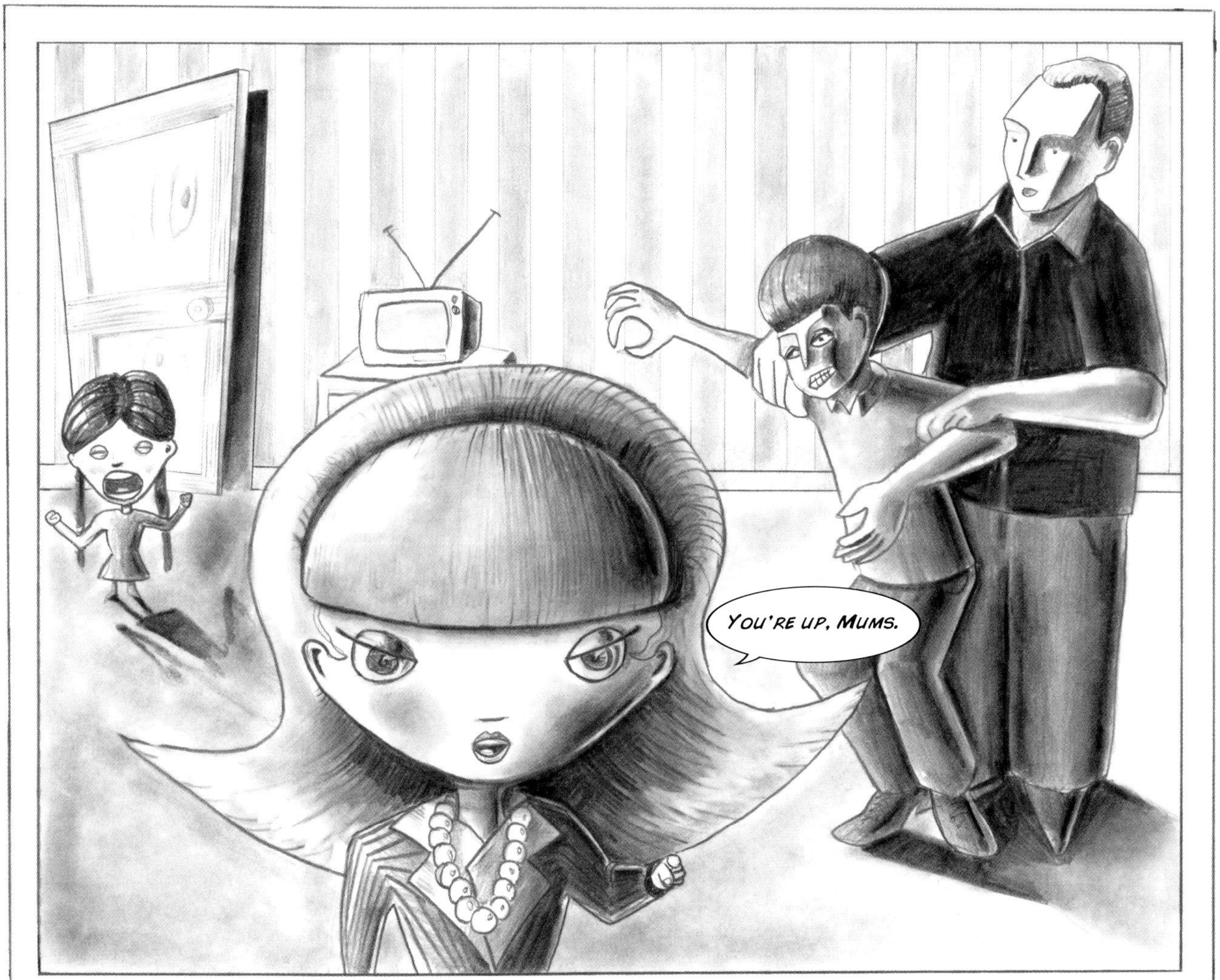
YOU'RE UP, MUMS.

Mummy's Sweet Cupcake is so insightful!

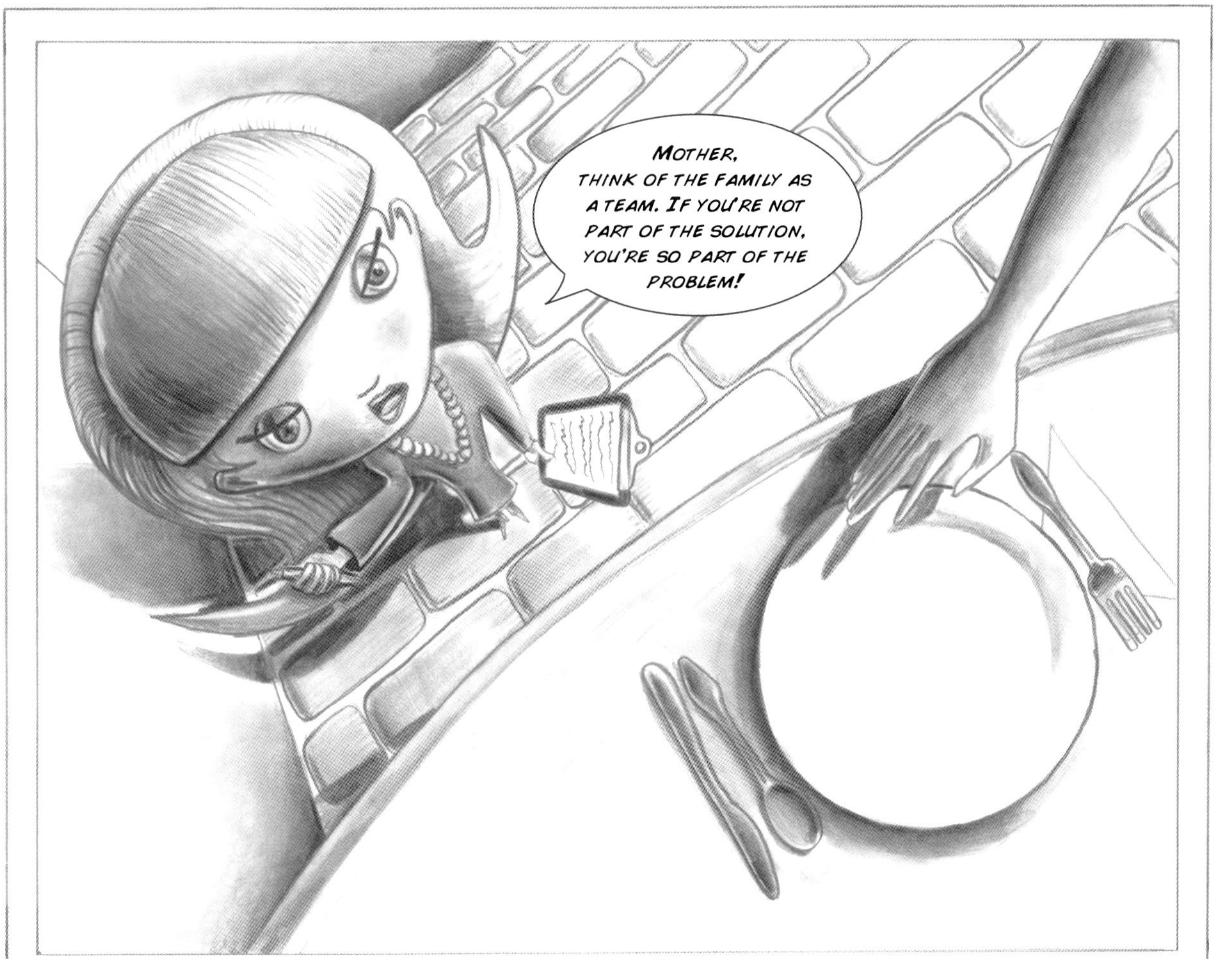
MOTHER,
THINK OF THE FAMILY AS
A TEAM. IF YOU'RE NOT
PART OF THE SOLUTION,
YOU'RE SO PART OF THE
PROBLEM!

And Dumpling just dotes on her Daddy!

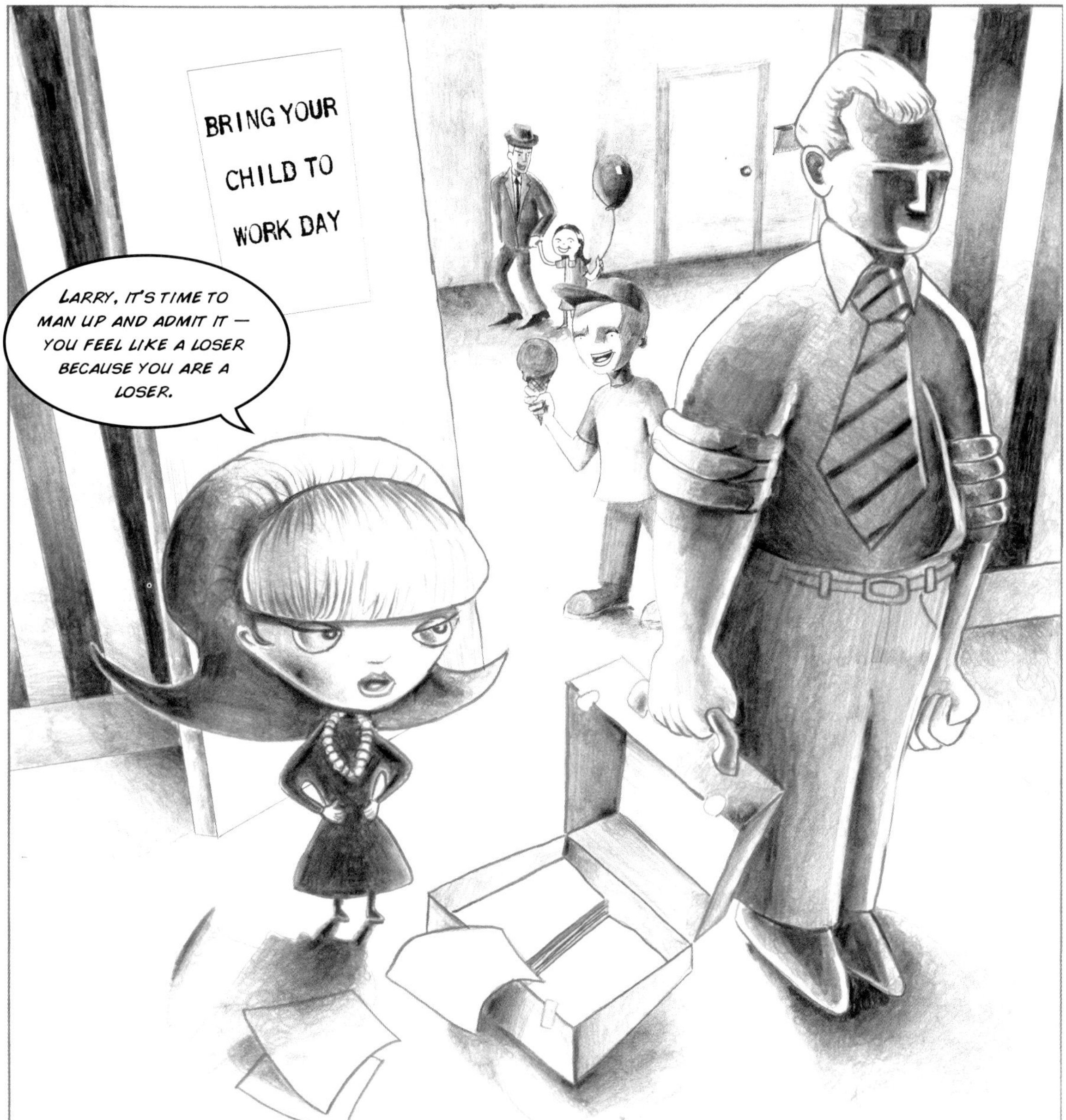
BRING YOUR CHILD TO WORK DAY
LARRY, IT'S TIME TO MAN UP AND ADMIT IT — YOU FEEL LIKE A LOSER BECAUSE YOU ARE A LOSER.

No one loved "chestnuts roasting on an open fire" time more than our Little Christmas Pudding.

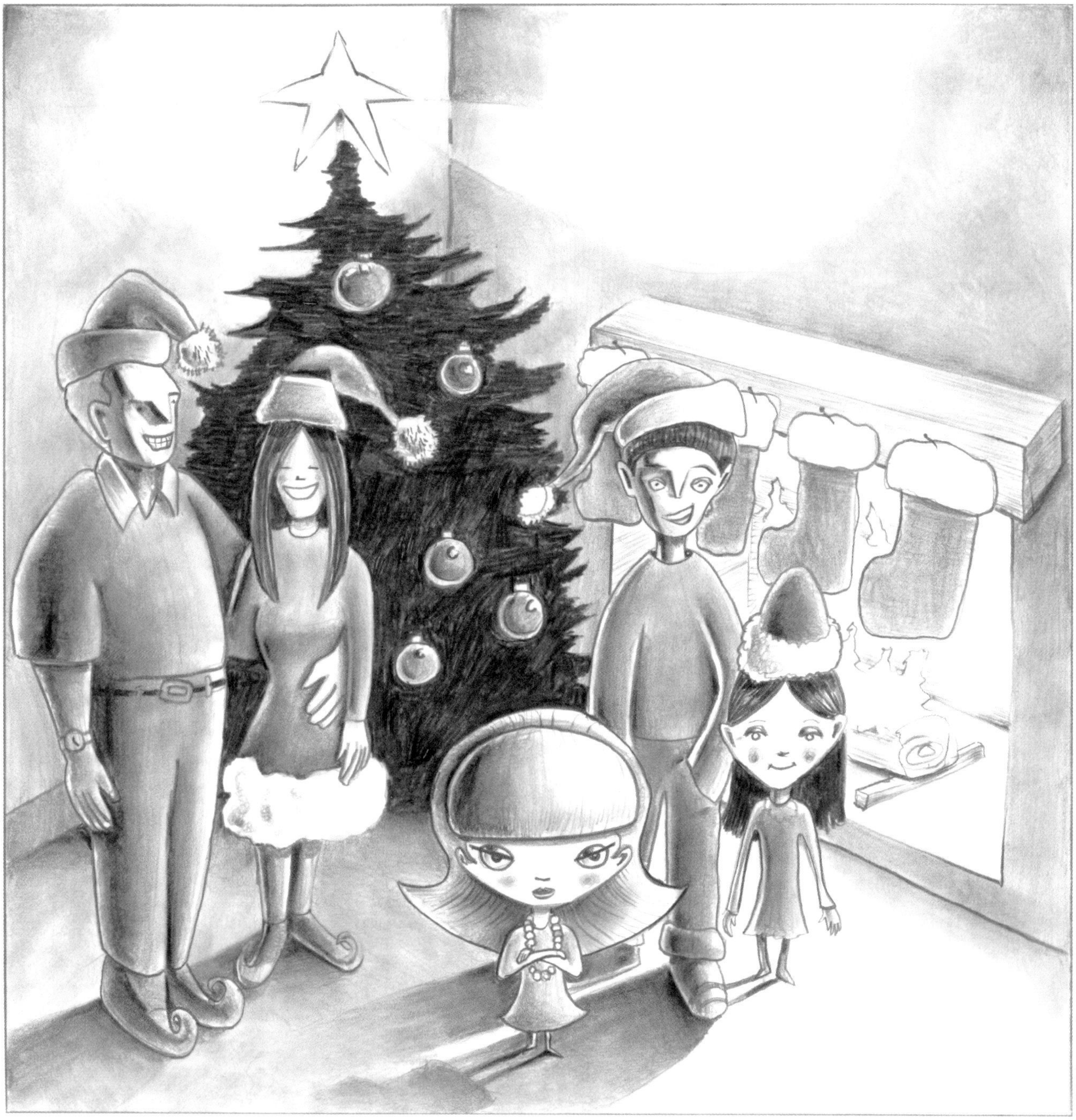

Note to self: Have all copies of this image incinerated
before Business Week profiles me on my first IPO.
– Isabel

Isabel loved playing with her siblings, and coyly teasing them.

As her brother and sister matured, however, Mummy's Little Chickadee didn't seem to grow an inch!

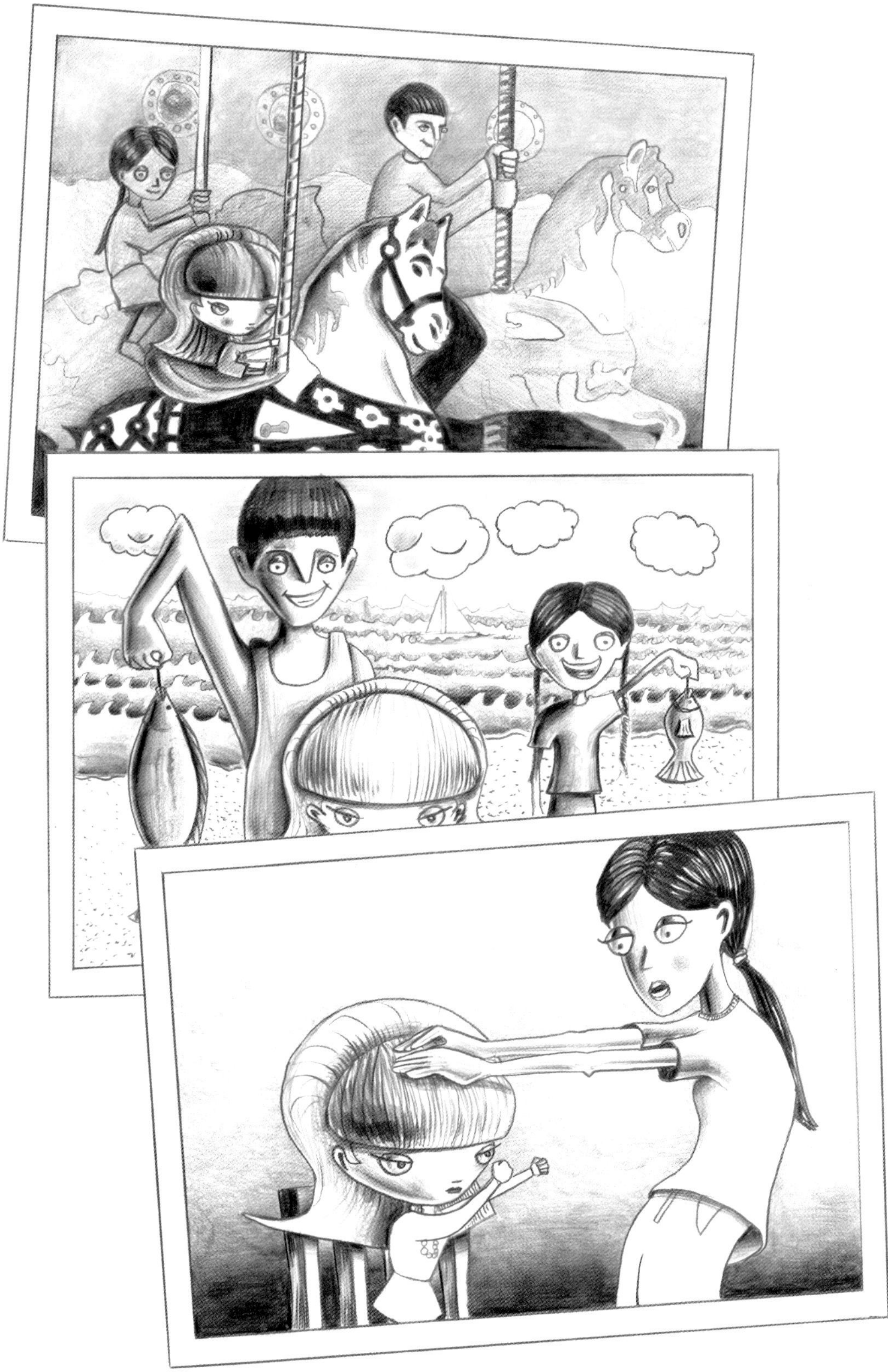

Me with the drooling cretins.
How could we possibly share the same genetic balance sheet?
Sis may be freakishly tall, but I call the shots in this family!

Even though our Little Princess was still five,
she insisted on having a social debut . . .
and I just couldn't say no.

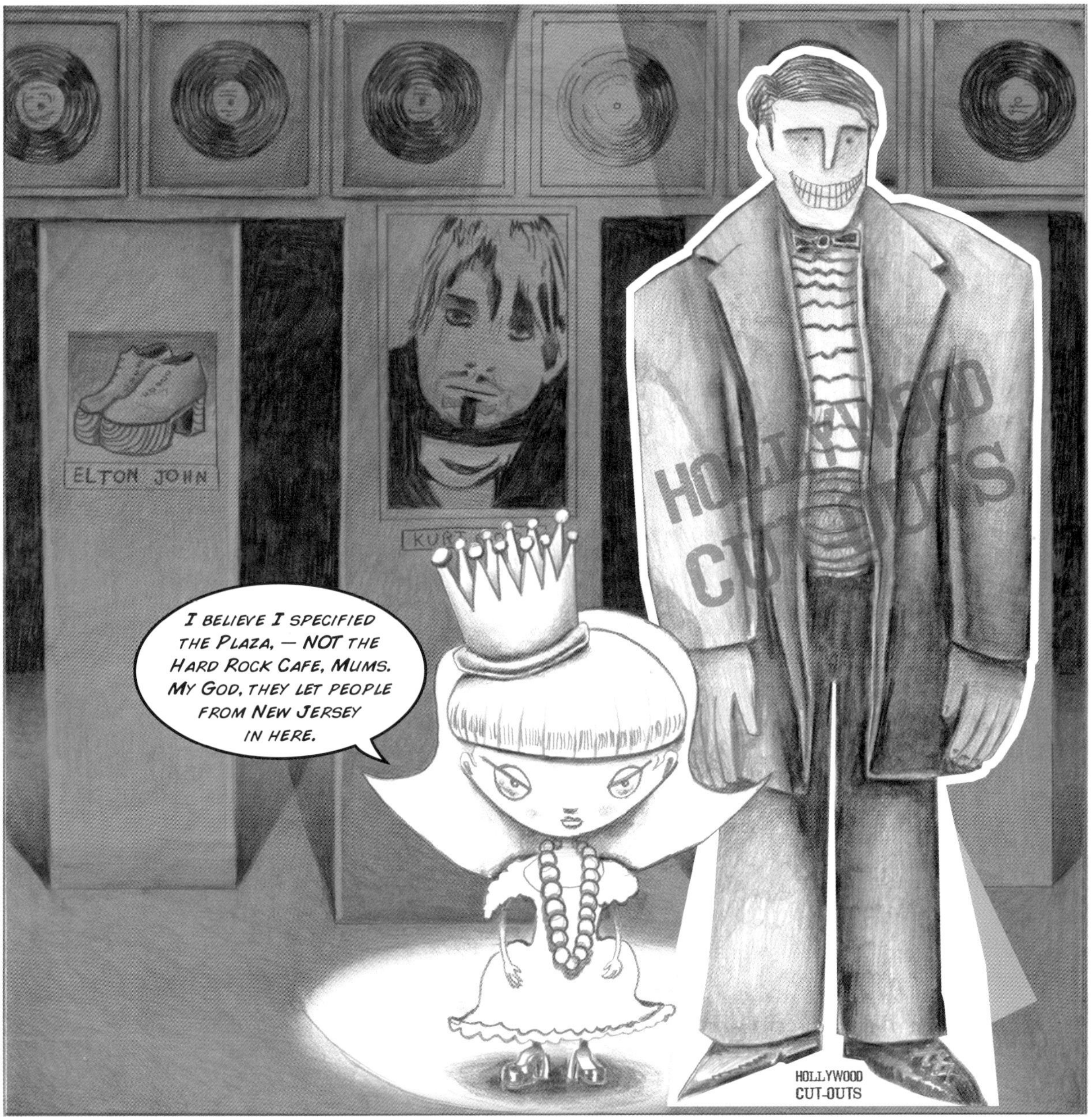
ELTON JOHN
KURT
I BELIEVE I SPECIFIED THE PLAZA, — NOT THE HARD ROCK CAFE, MUMS. MY GOD, THEY LET PEOPLE FROM NEW JERSEY IN HERE.
HOLLYWOOD CUT-OUTS

Isabel's trip to the zoo with Uncle Tim did not go well, especially after he presented her with a horrid stuffed animal instead of what she really wanted . . .

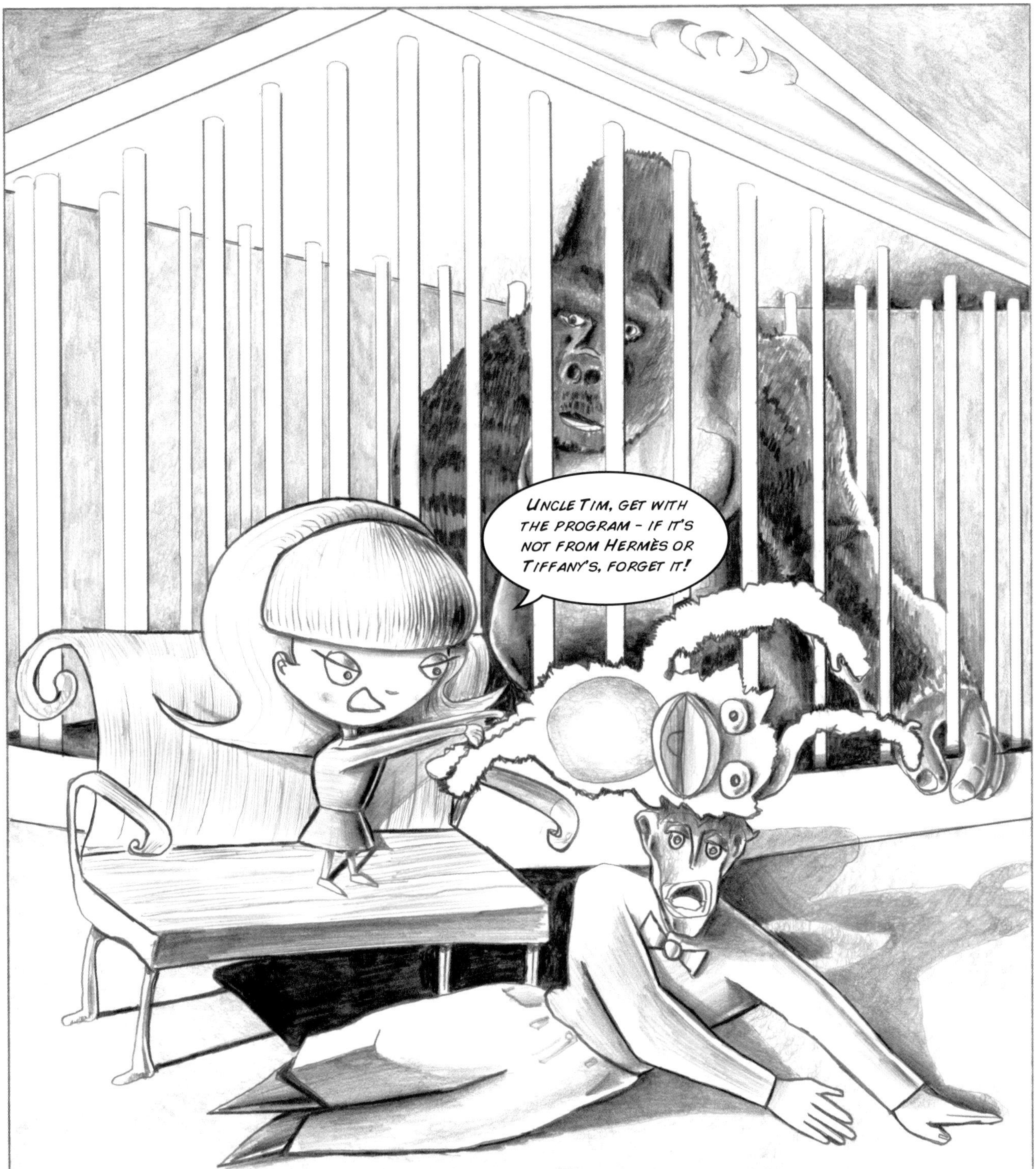
UNCLE TIM, GET WITH THE PROGRAM - IF IT'S NOT FROM HERMÈS OR TIFFANY'S, FORGET IT!

Of course, Mummy almost had a fit when she learned Isabel was sneaking into the Singles Scene. I grounded her! I know the library isn't open till one in the a.m.!

I guess Baby just craved attention because she witnessed the bliss Mummy and Daddy enjoy together.

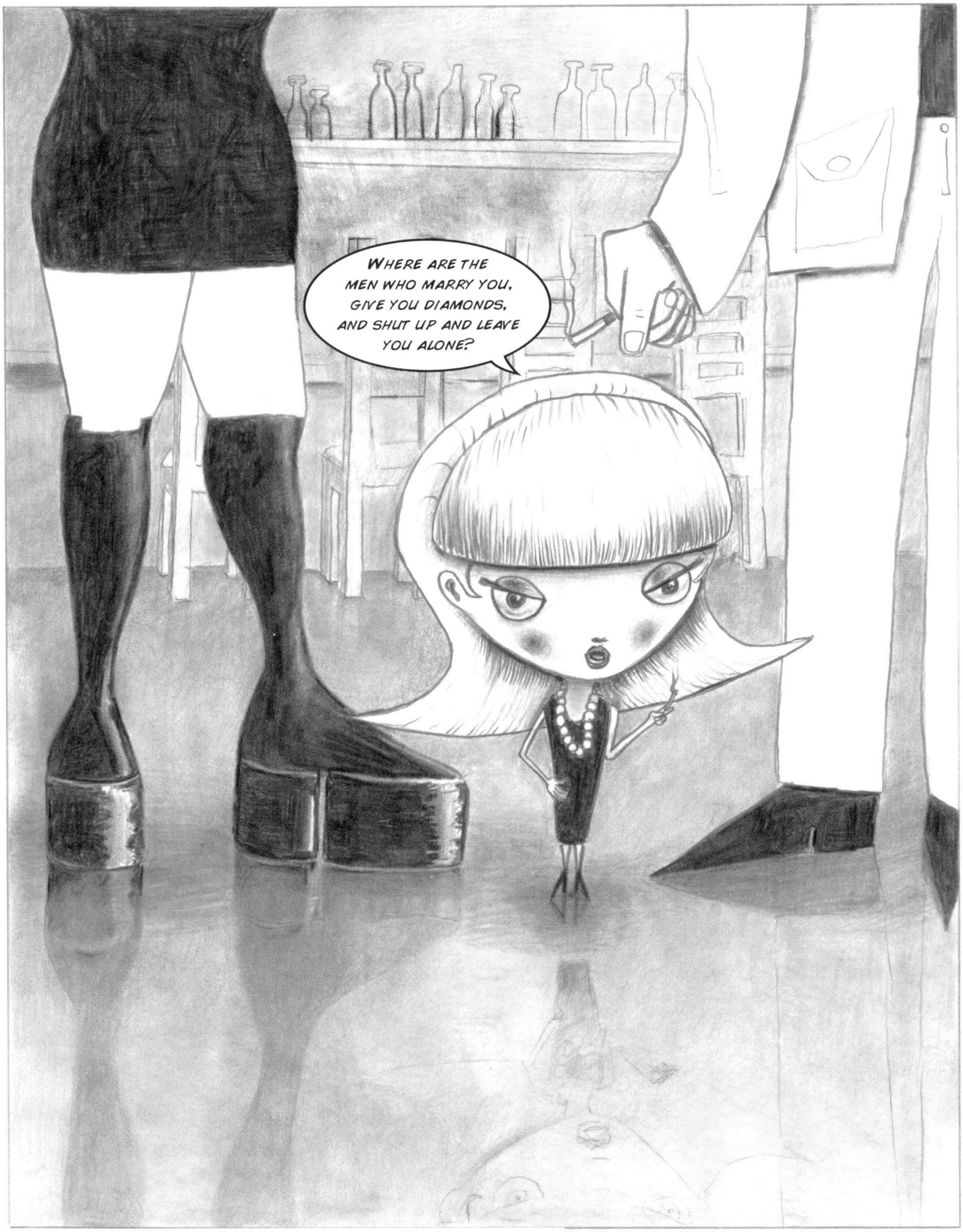
WHERE ARE THE MEN WHO MARRY YOU, GIVE YOU DIAMONDS, AND SHUT UP AND LEAVE YOU ALONE?

Little Isabel loved the spotlight and Mummy encouraged our Little Diva's desire to be center stage.

She had a bit of an awkward start — her debut in an avant-garde production of *Sound of Music* was ill-conceived.

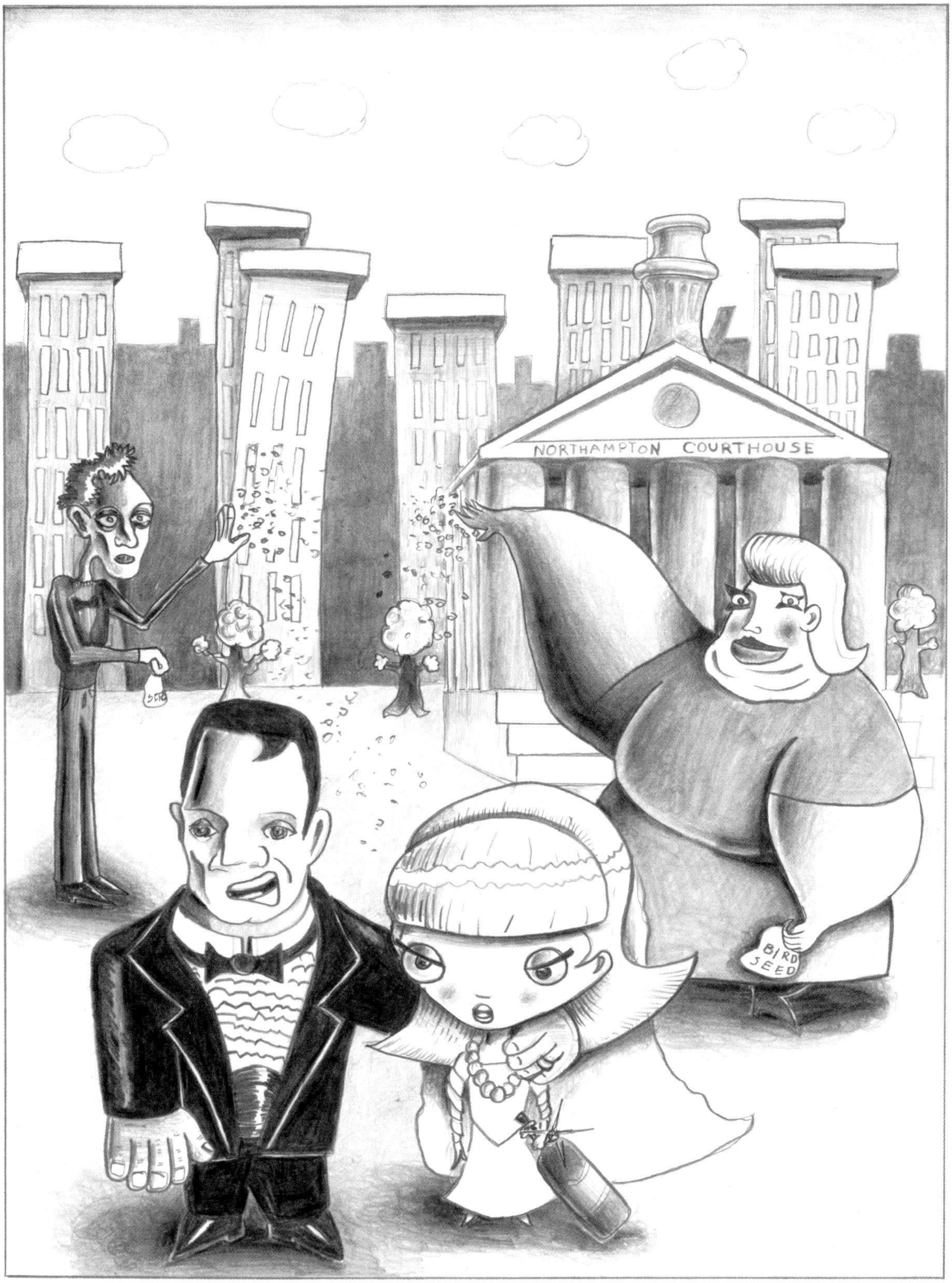
NORTHAMPTON COURTHOUSE
BIRD SEED

But by the time she gave her first commencement speech – even though, technically, she wasn't invited – there was no stopping her. She literally stole the show!

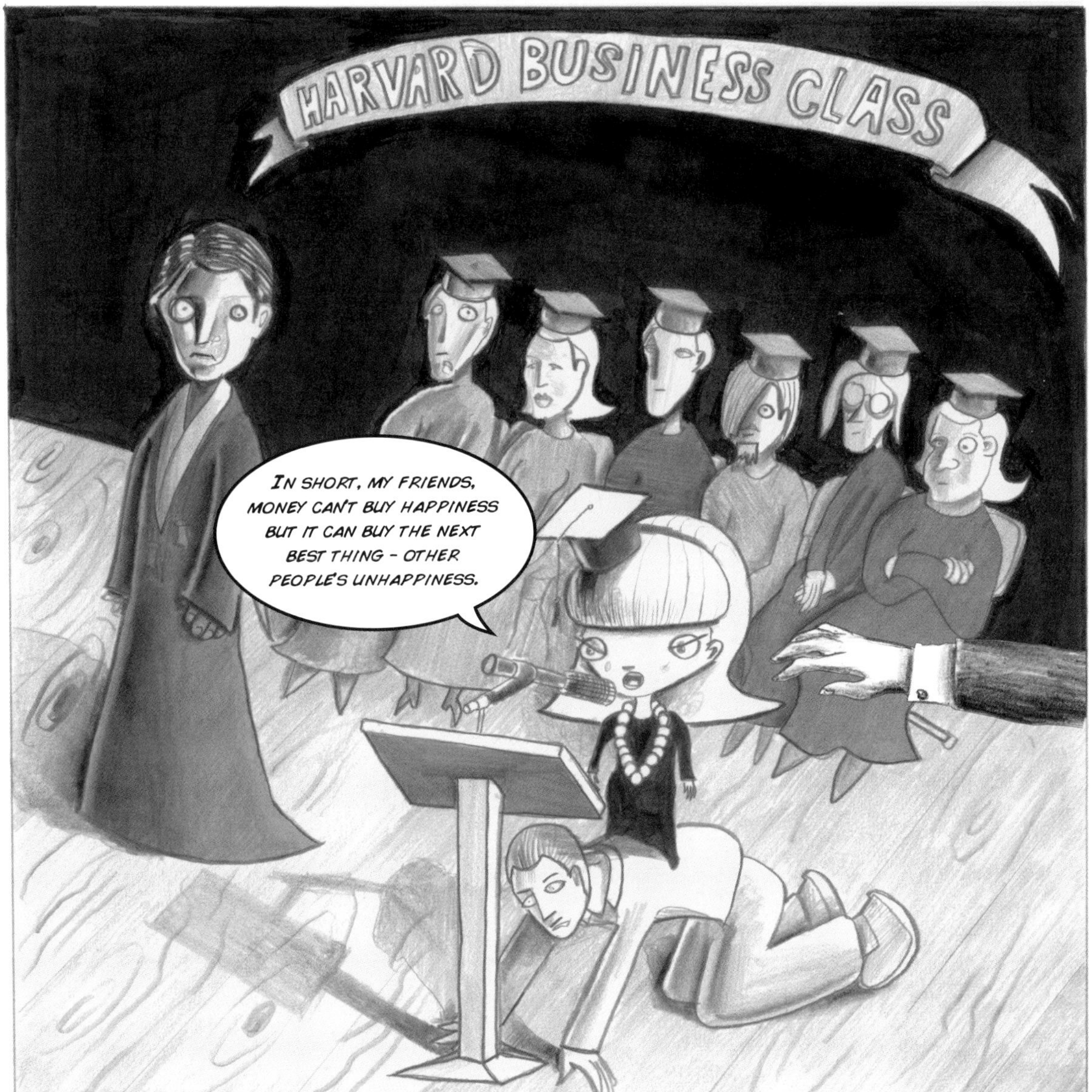
HARVARD BUSINESS CLASS
IN SHORT, MY FRIENDS, MONEY CAN'T BUY HAPPINESS BUT IT CAN BUY THE NEXT BEST THING - OTHER PEOPLE'S UNHAPPINESS.

Not one to rest on her well-earned achievements, Isabel made quite an impression at Daddy's annual office party.

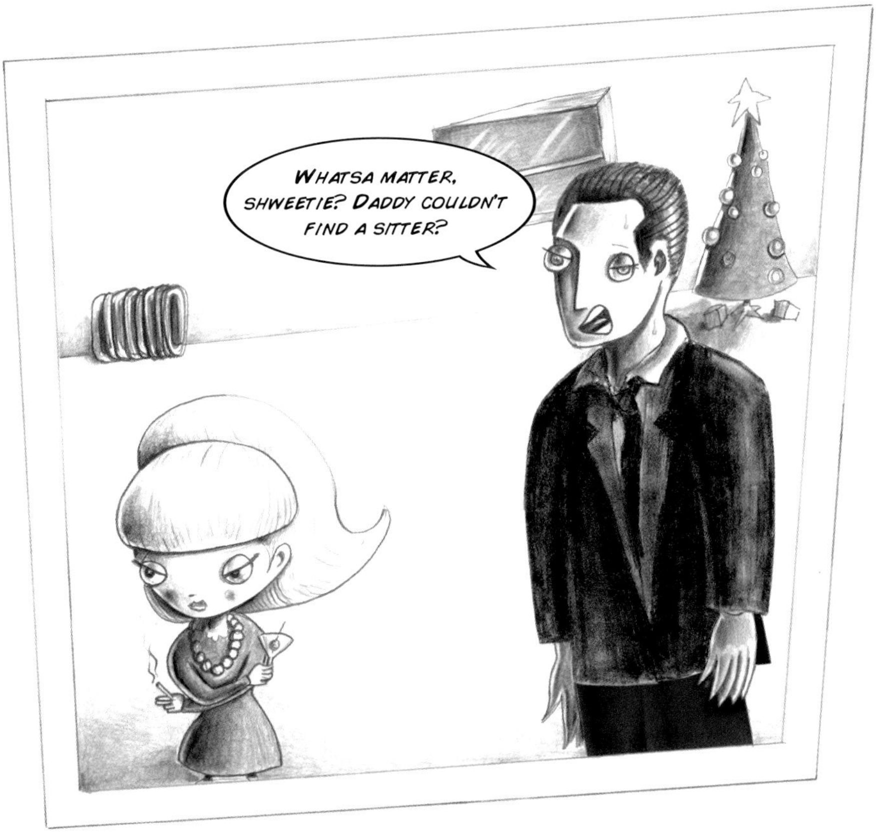
WHATSA MATTER, SHWEETIE? DADDY COULDN'T FIND A SITTER?

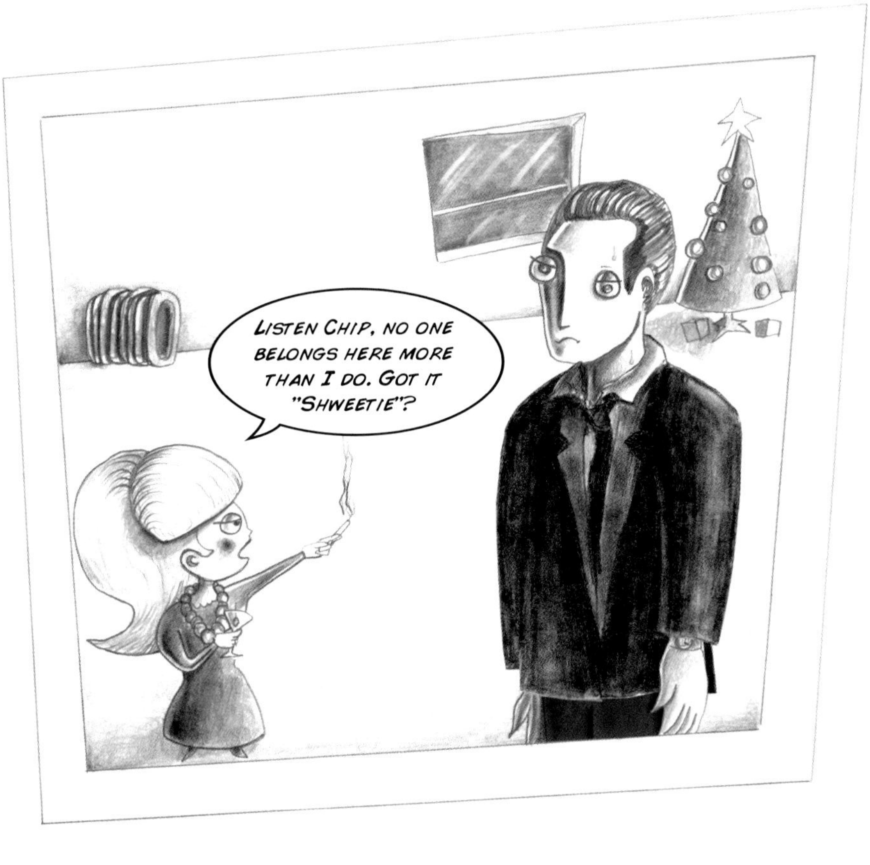
LISTEN CHIP, NO ONE BELONGS HERE MORE THAN I DO. GOT IT "SHWEETIE"?

In no time at all, Mummy's Girl Genius was well on her way to the corner office. Everyone was so impressed they didn't even question her as she — what did she call it? — "began to execute new synergies and efficiencies."

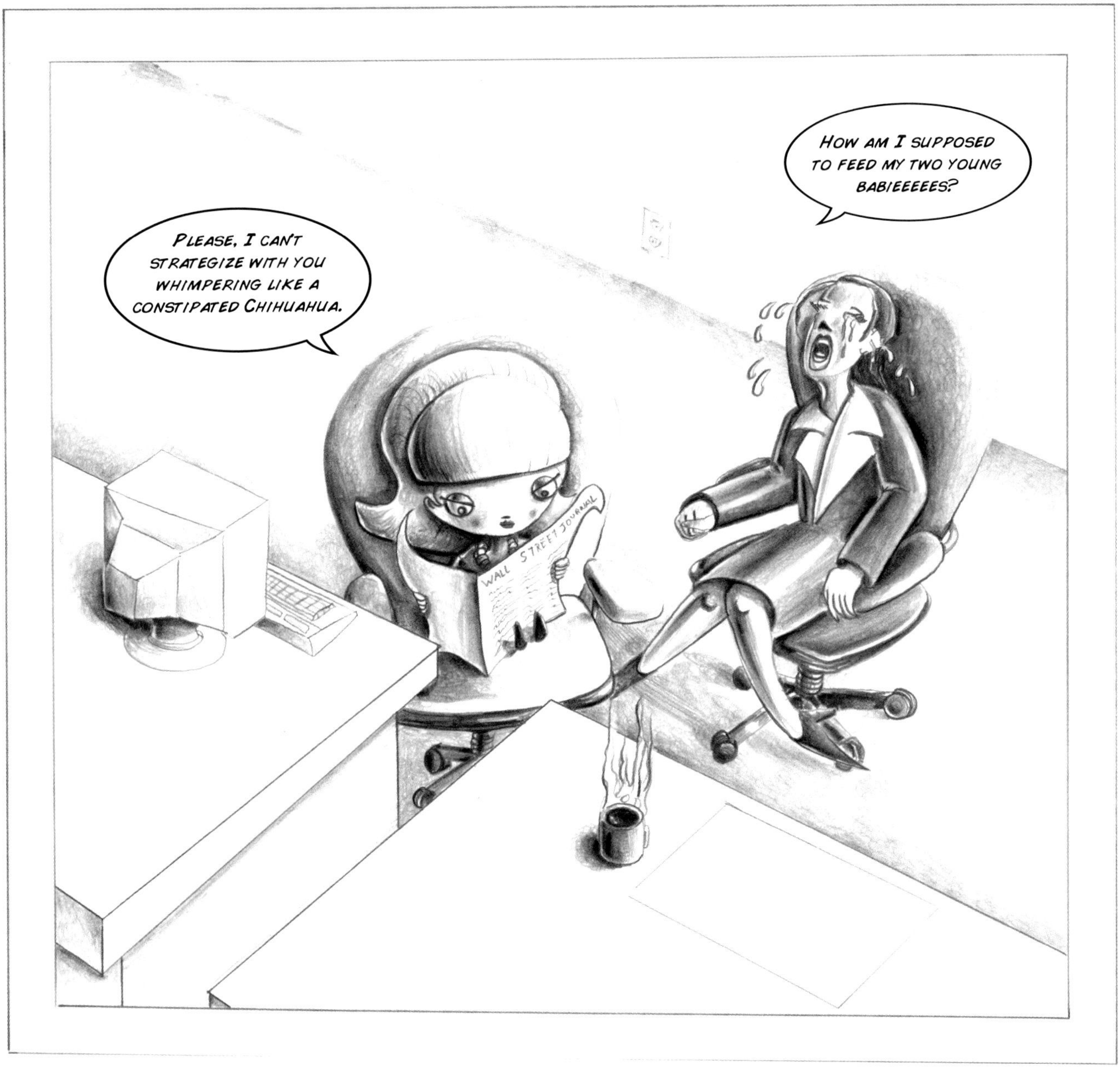

HOW AM I SUPPOSED TO FEED MY TWO YOUNG BABIEEEEES?
PLEASE, I CAN'T STRATEGIZE WITH YOU WHIMPERING LIKE A CONSTIPATED CHIHUAHUA.
WALL STREET JOURNAL

At times, I know Isabel felt like she was carrying the weight of the world on her shoulders.

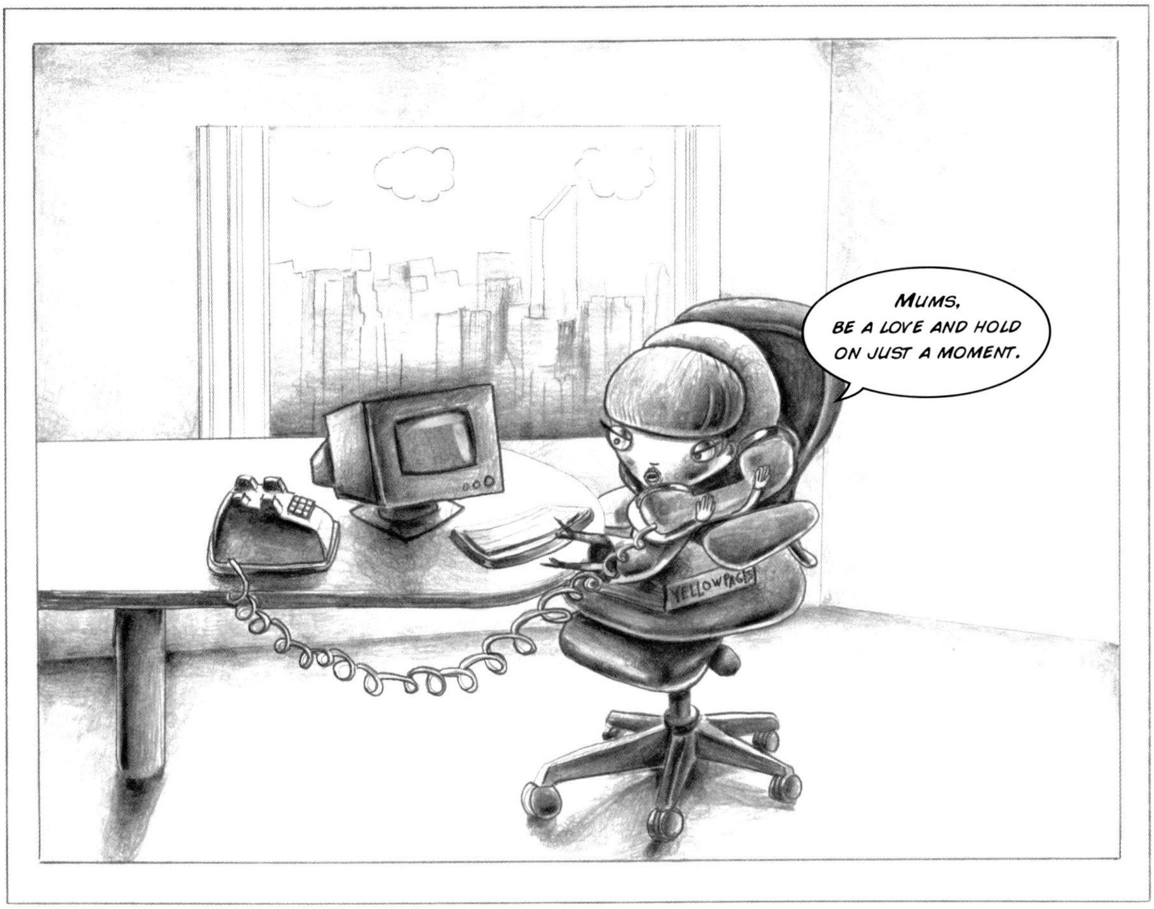
MUMS, BE A LOVE AND HOLD ON JUST A MOMENT.

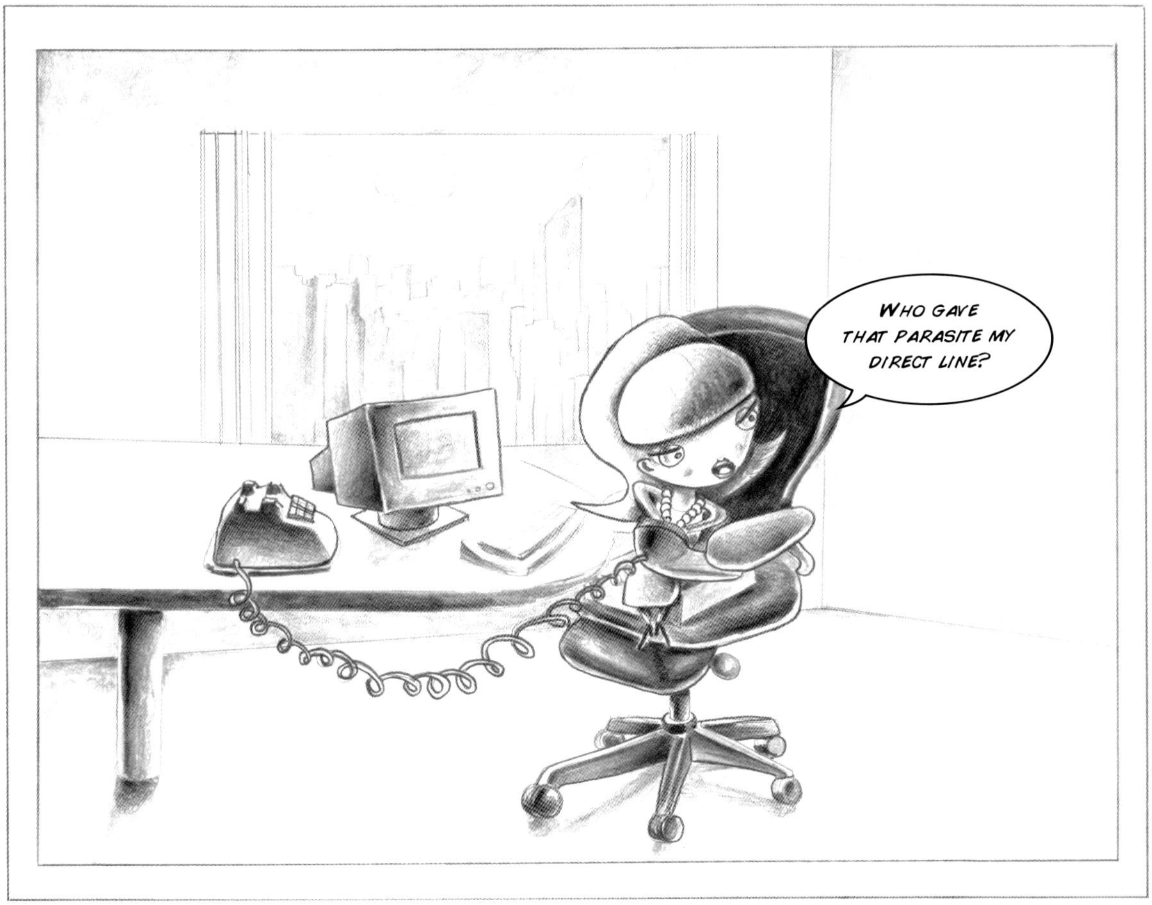
WHO GAVE THAT PARASITE MY DIRECT LINE?

But no matter how busy our Cuddly Little CEO was, she always had time for her beloved niece and nephew.

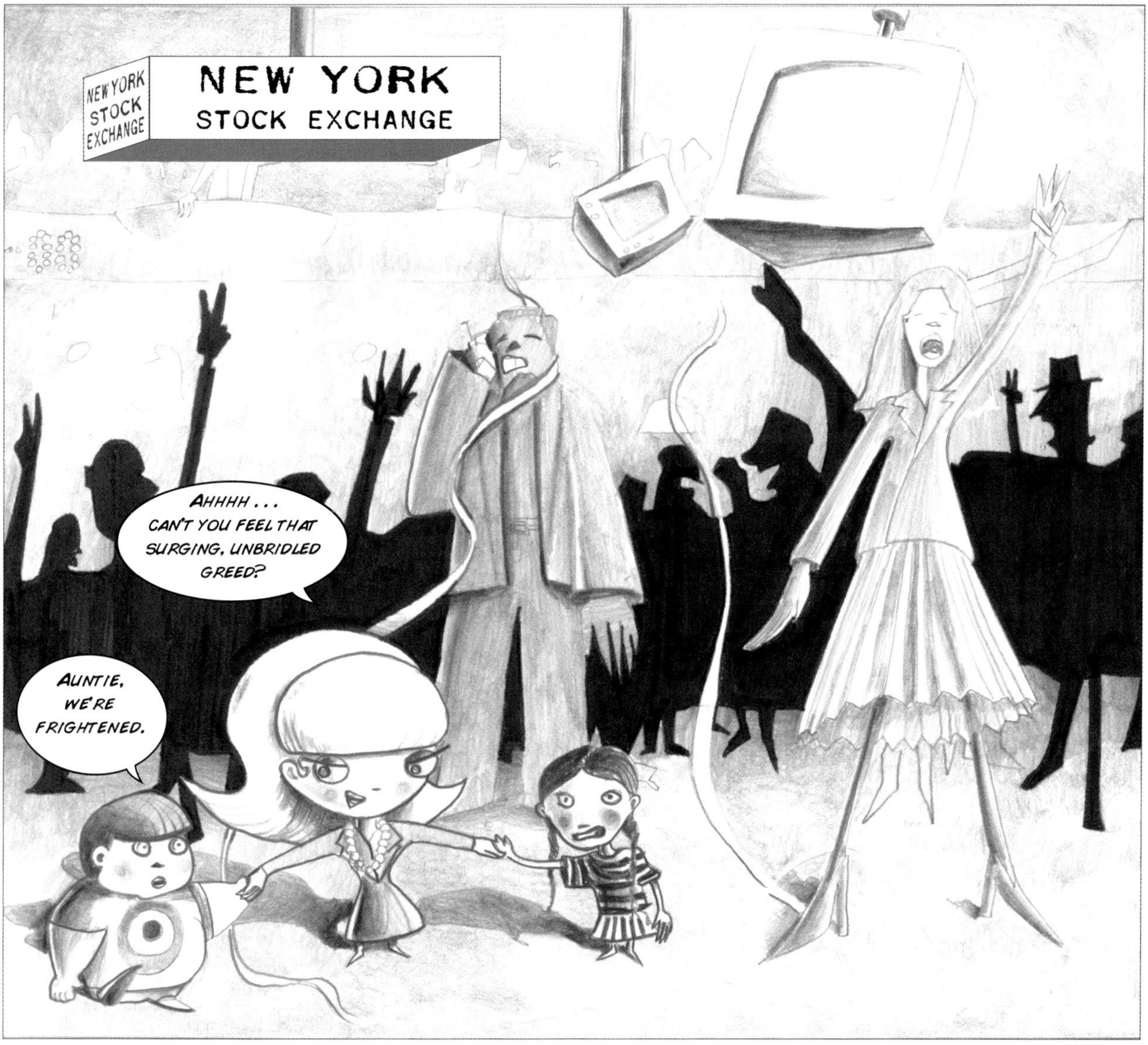
NEW YORK STOCK EXCHANGE
NEW YORK
STOCK EXCHANGE
AHHHH . . . CAN'T YOU FEEL THAT SURGING, UNBRIDLED GREED?
AUNTIE, WE'RE FRIGHTENED.

Isabel had found her place at the
top of the heap.

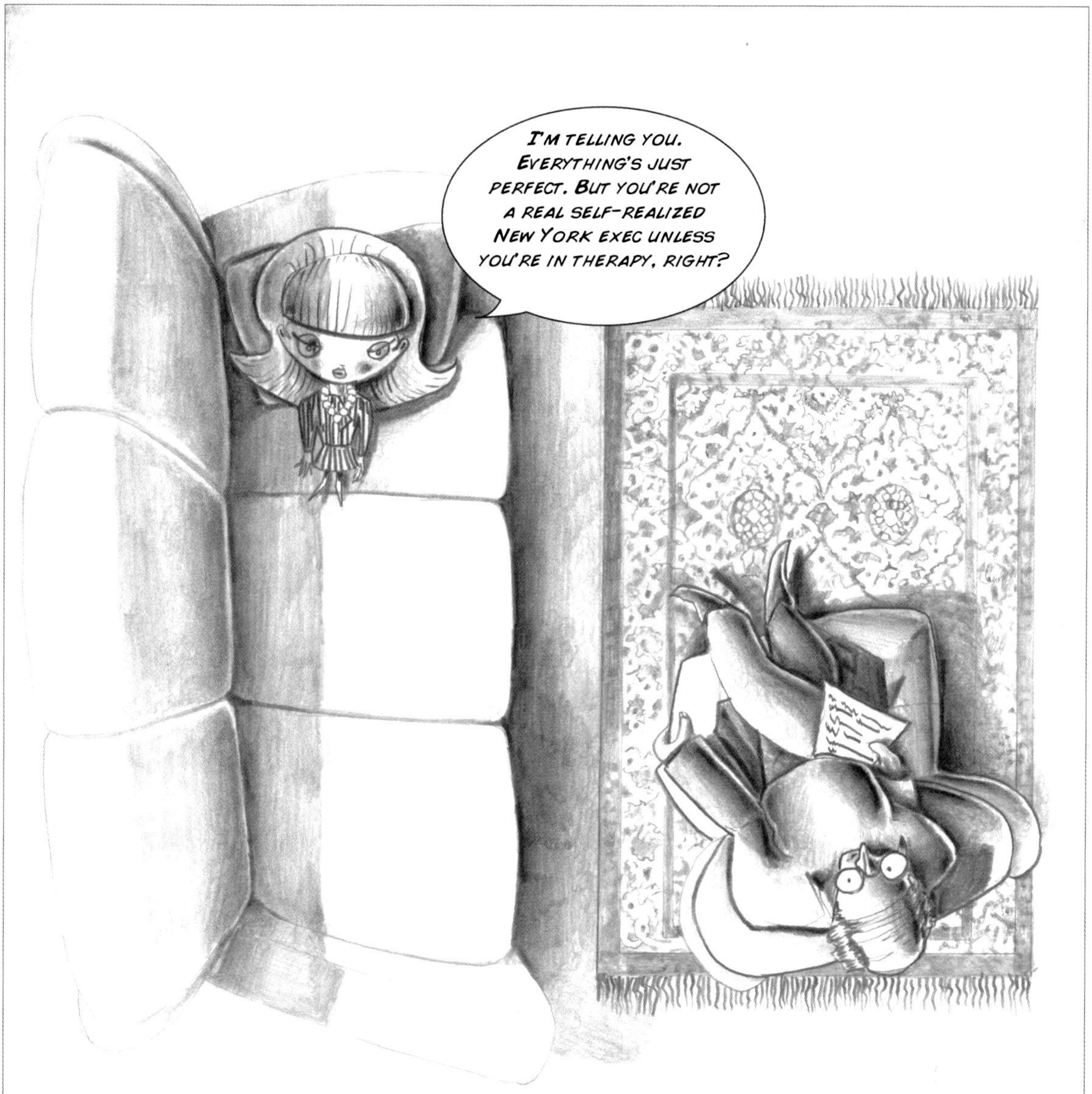
I'M TELLING YOU. EVERYTHING'S JUST PERFECT. BUT YOU'RE NOT A REAL SELF-REALIZED NEW YORK EXEC UNLESS YOU'RE IN THERAPY, RIGHT?

Then something a tad peculiar started happening: Just at the point Isabel reached the tippy-top height of her career . . .

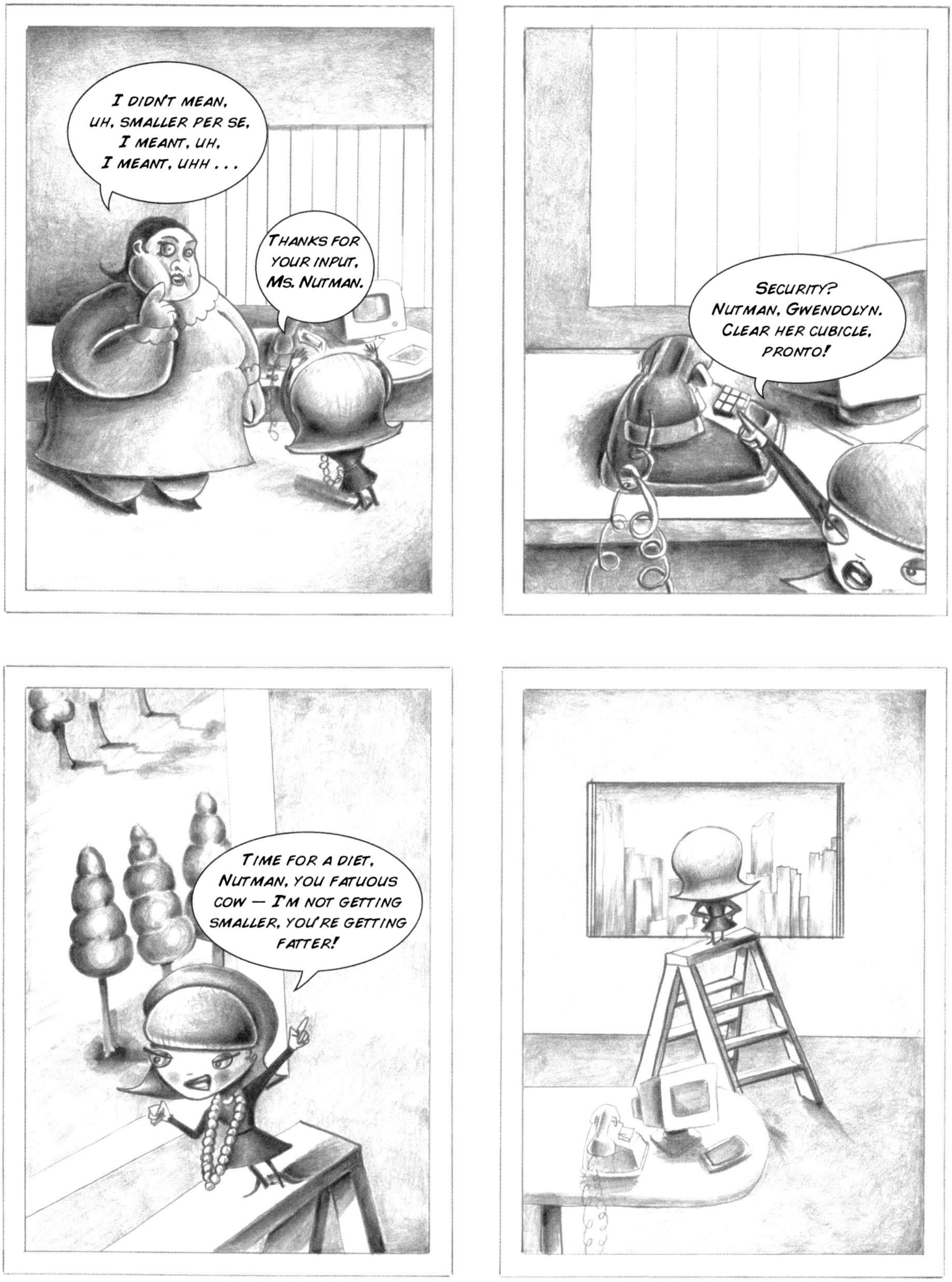
I DIDN'T MEAN, UH, SMALLER PER SE, I MEANT, UH, I MEANT, UHH . . .
THANKS FOR YOUR INPUT, MS. NUTMAN.
SECURITY? NUTMAN, GWENDOLYN. CLEAR HER CUBICLE, PRONTO!
TIME FOR A DIET, NUTMAN, YOU FATUOUS COW — I'M NOT GETTING SMALLER, YOU'RE GETTING FATTER!

just as she reached a professional pinnacle . . .
she began to shrink.

I SAID, BRING ME ONE IN MY SIZE! FOCUS, PEOPLE!

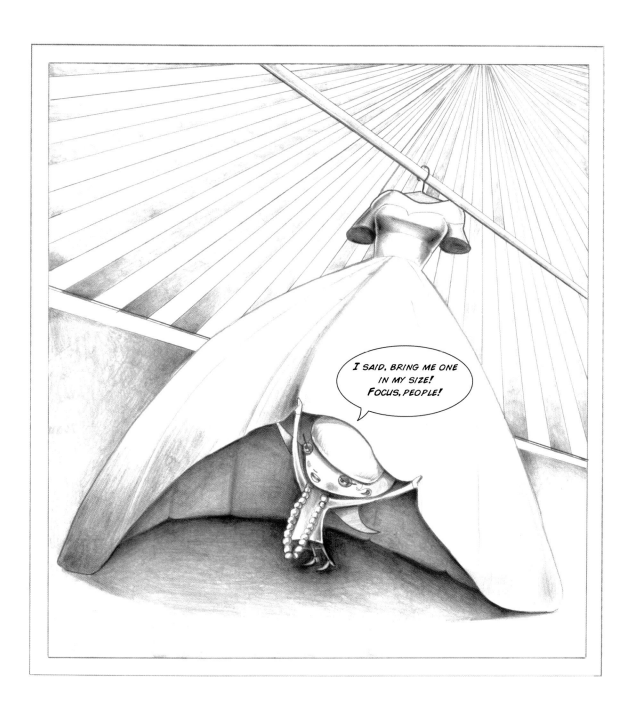

Mummy's Precious Wonder didn't let a little thing like that get in her way. She had found her place in the world.

Still, people didn't seem to take Isabel quite as seriously as she wanted them to.

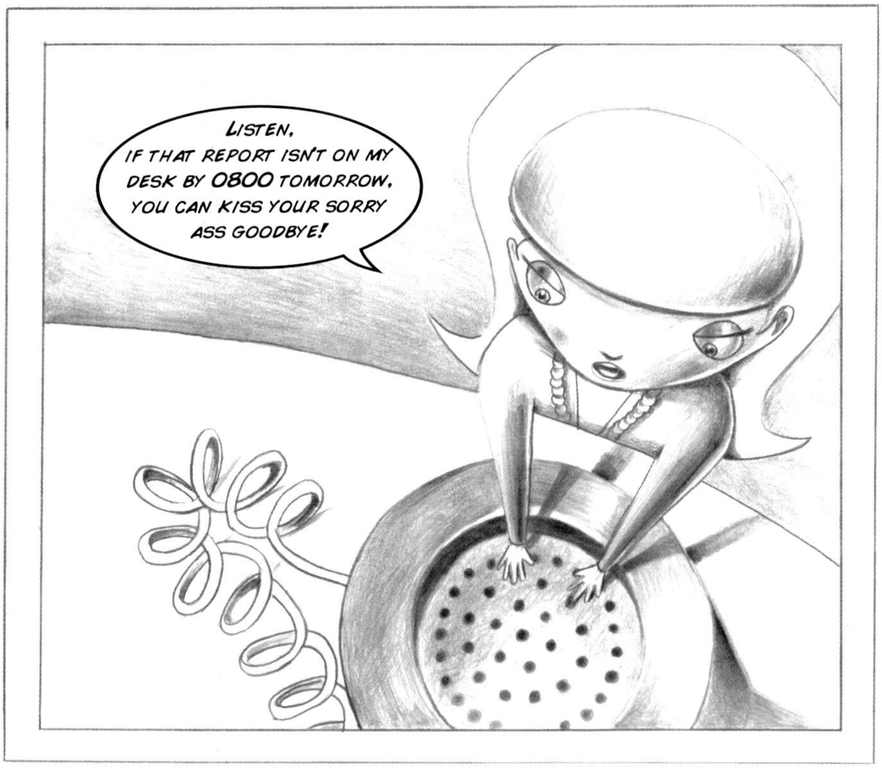
LISTEN,
IF THAT REPORT ISN'T ON MY DESK BY 0800 TOMORROW, YOU CAN KISS YOUR SORRY ASS GOODBYE!

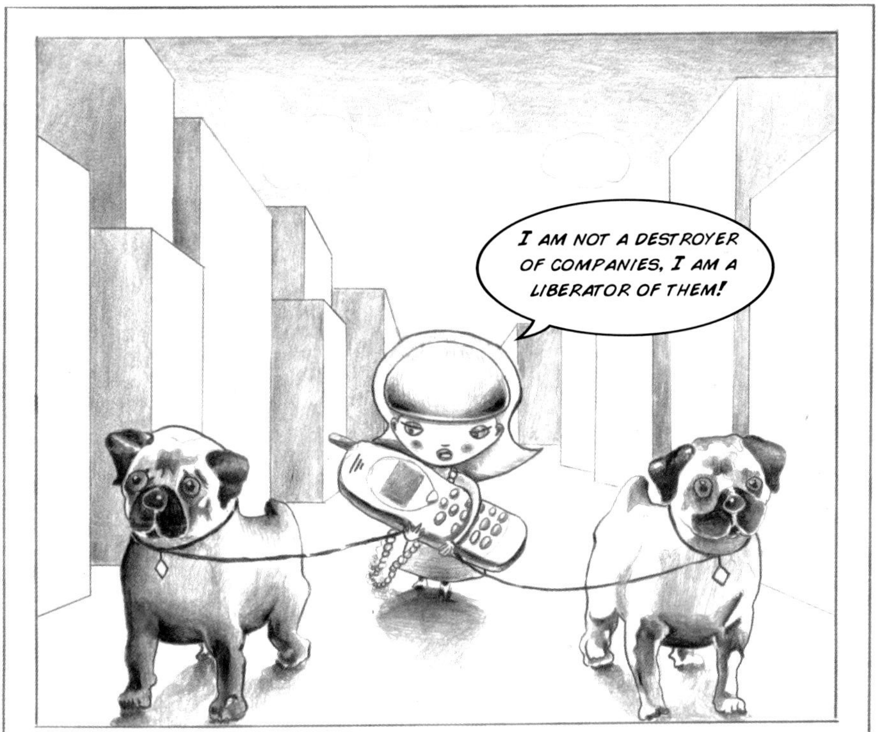
I AM NOT A DESTROYER OF COMPANIES. I AM A LIBERATOR OF THEM!

The rank and file that once feared Isabel were now turning on her. It seems the board of directors found it difficult bending to the will of a feisty five-year-old weighing all of fourteen pounds (jewelry included).

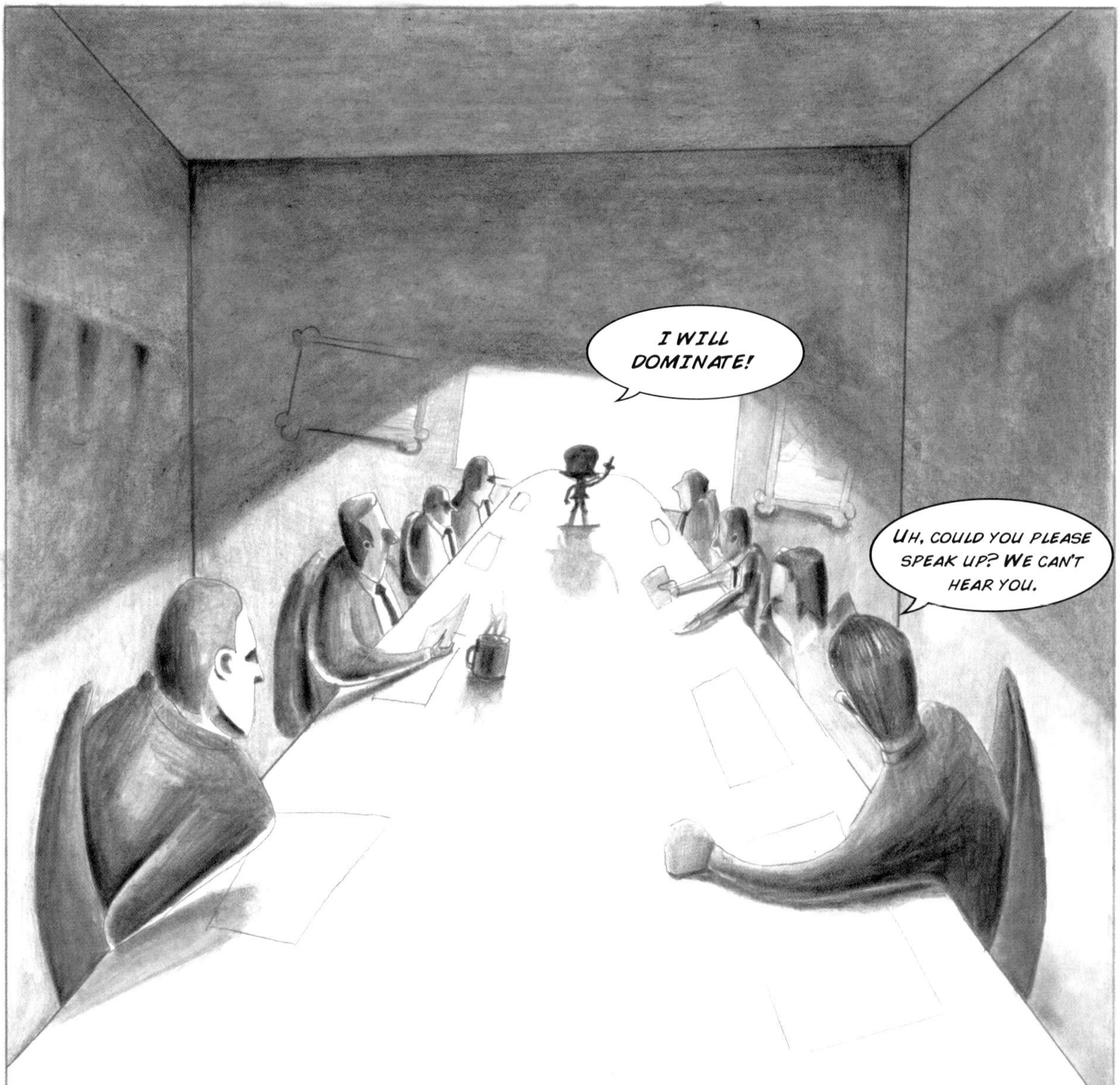
I WILL DOMINATE!
UH, COULD YOU PLEASE SPEAK UP? WE CAN'T HEAR YOU.

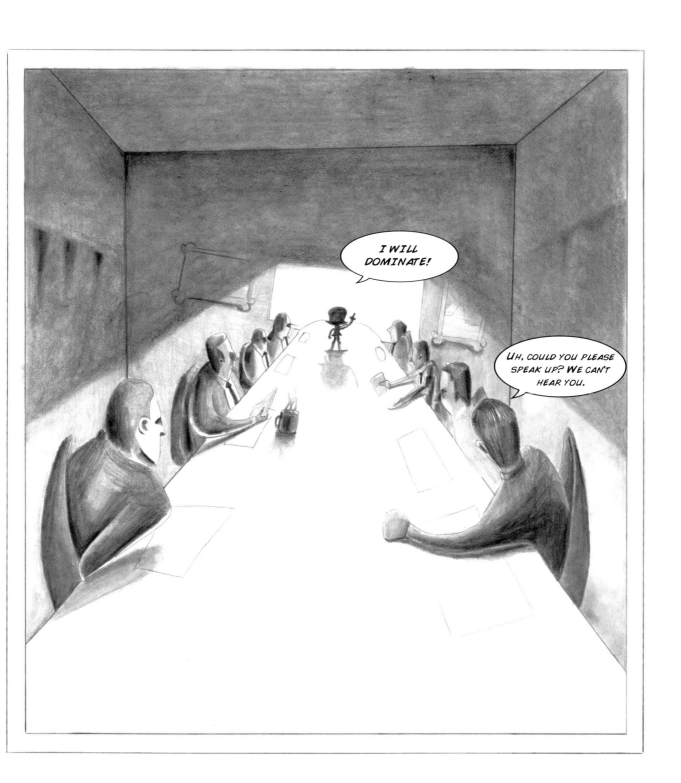

The board dispatched the company's dedicated nest of writhing vipers to strike a killing blow . . . the Human Resources Co-Heads.

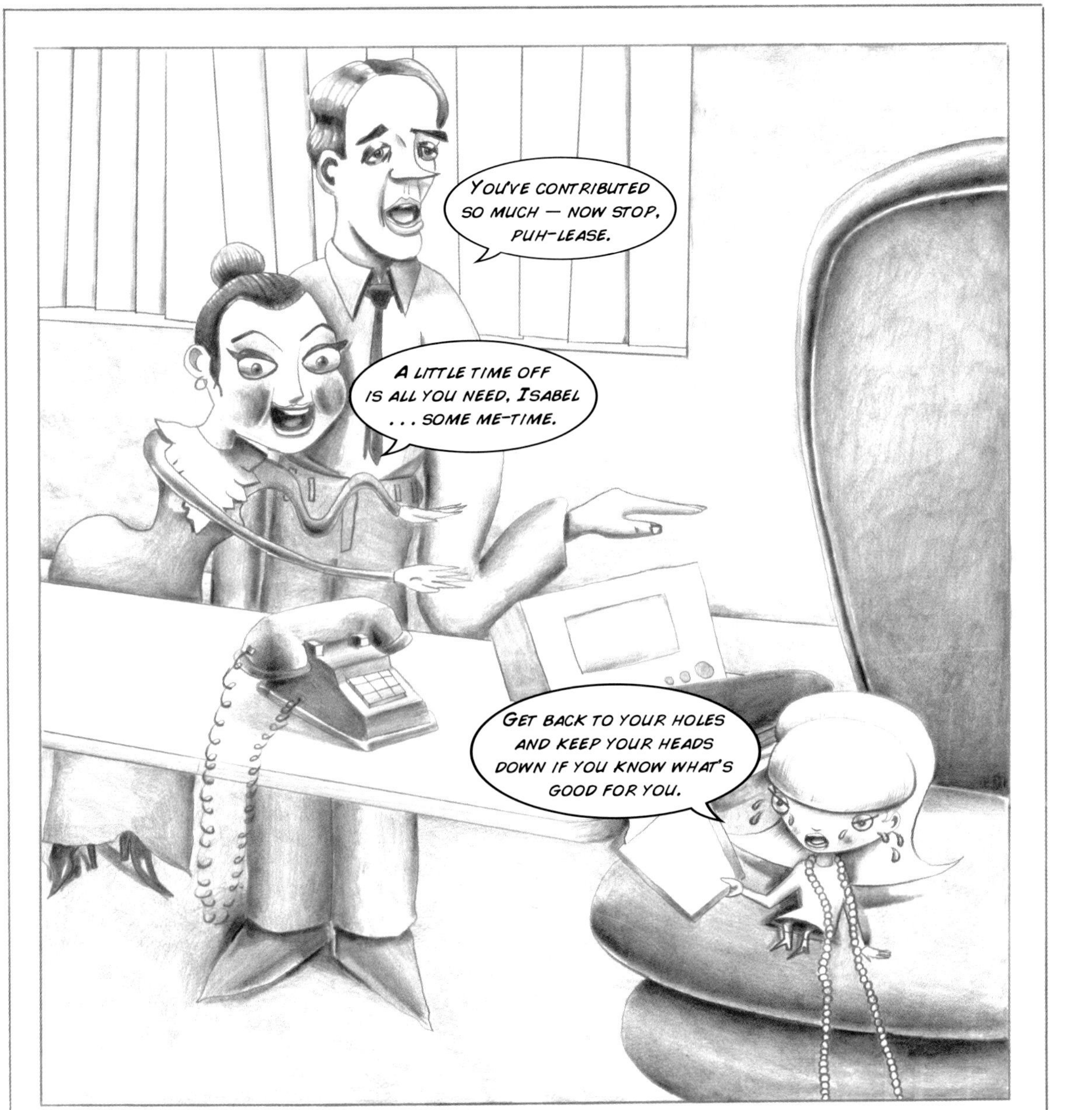
YOU'VE CONTRIBUTED SO MUCH — NOW STOP, PUH-LEASE.
A LITTLE TIME OFF IS ALL YOU NEED, ISABEL . . . SOME ME-TIME.
GET BACK TO YOUR HOLES AND KEEP YOUR HEADS DOWN IF YOU KNOW WHAT'S GOOD FOR YOU.

I don't know why, but as Isabel clung more and more tightly to her dream, she seemed to get even smaller. Could Mummy have helped? I honestly don't know.

She started seeing that quack again.

Four times.

A week.

But as she continued to shrink, her anxiety grew.

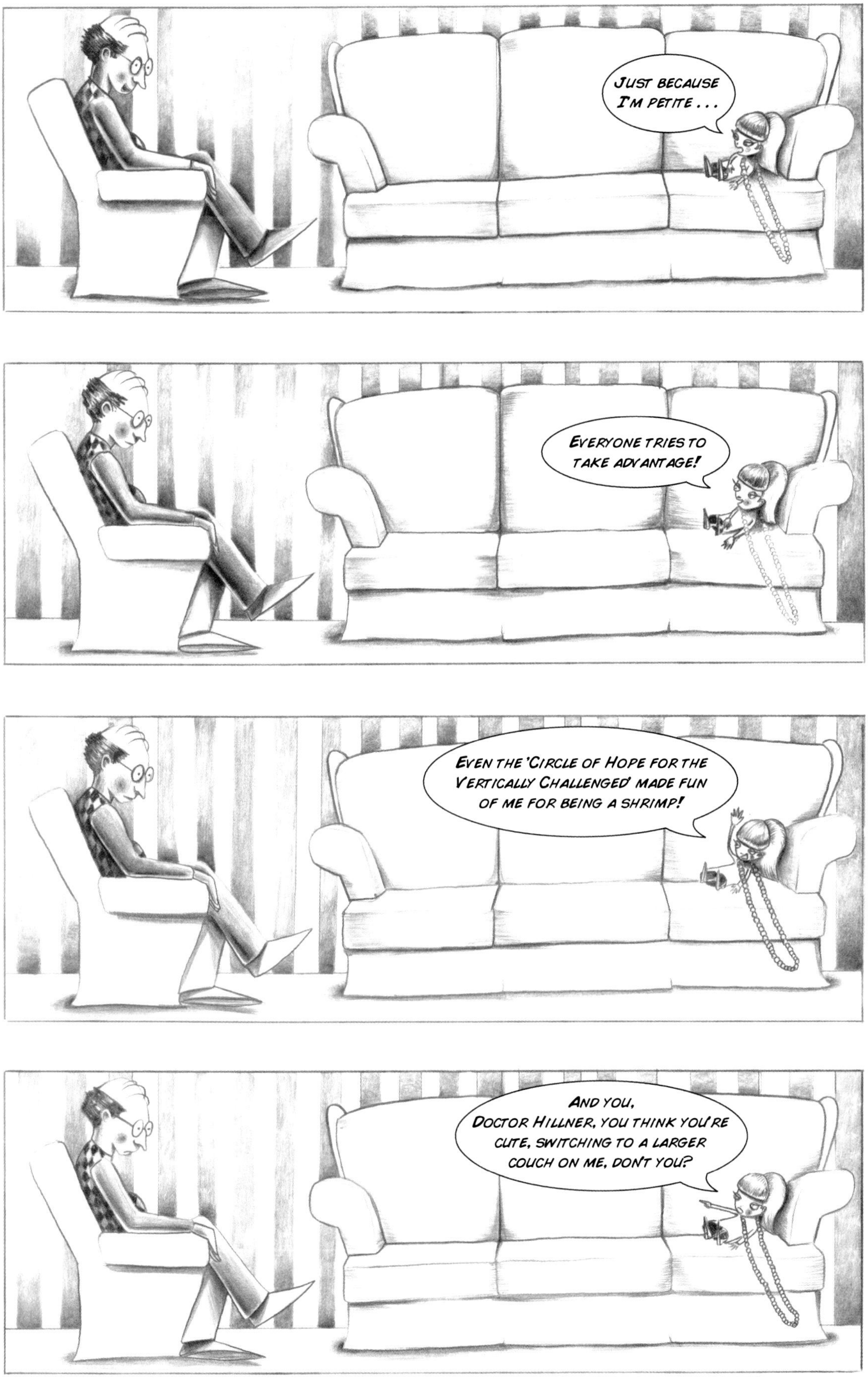
Just because I'm petite . . .
Everyone tries to take advantage!
Even the 'Circle of Hope for the Vertically Challenged' made fun of me for being a shrimp!
And you, Doctor Hillner, you think you're cute, switching to a larger couch on me, don't you?

I fully supported her decision
to stay the course.

Isabel threw herself into her work, bless her, at
the office round the clock, not returning calls.

Not even when Mummy pretended
to be Martha Stewart.

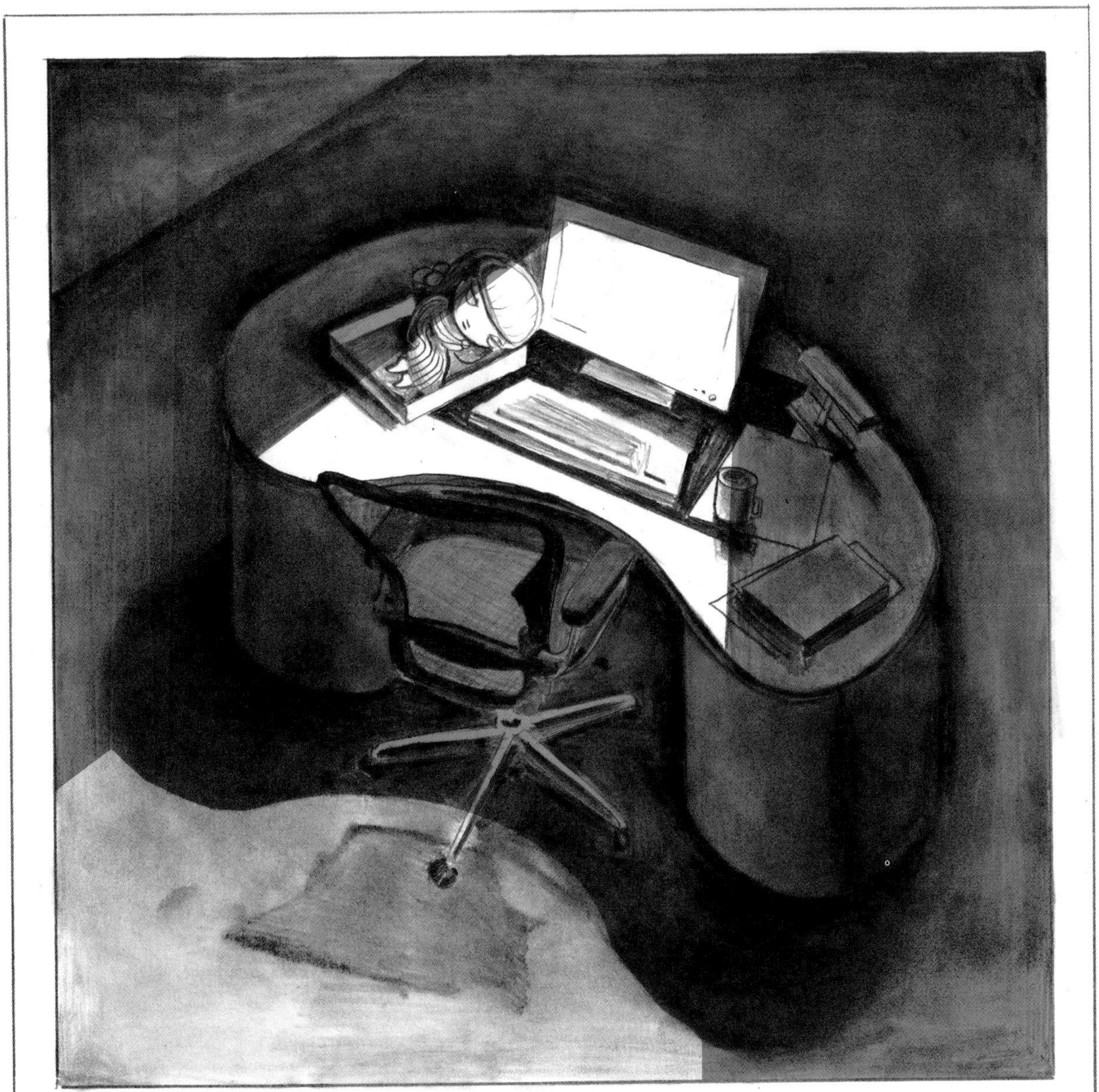

At times she surprised me. Even when no one lifted a finger to help her — except her beloved Mummy, of course — Isabel continued to give and give.

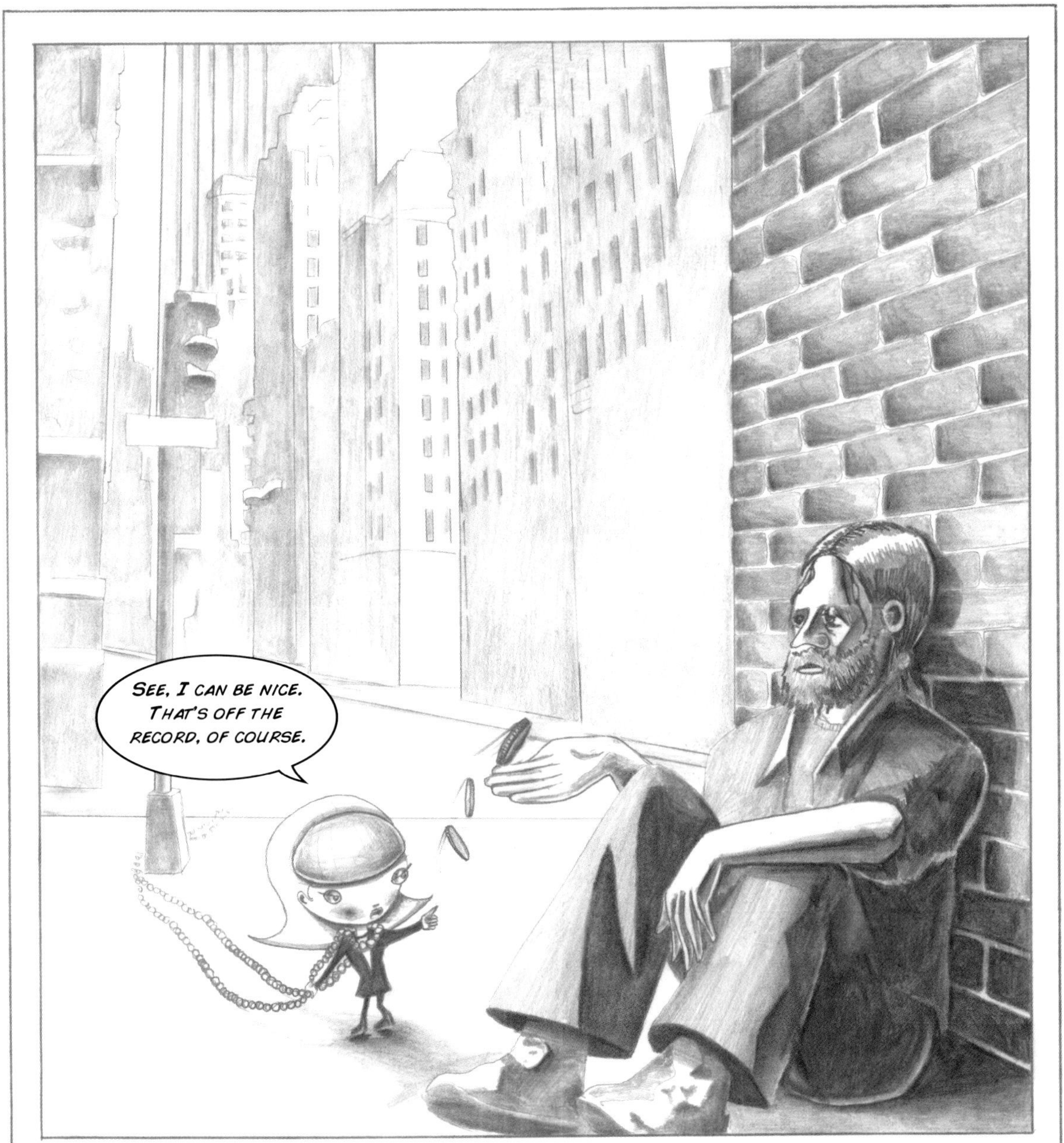
SEE, I CAN BE NICE. THAT'S OFF THE RECORD, OF COURSE.

Say what you will — Isabel never backed down when it came to playing hardball with the big boys.

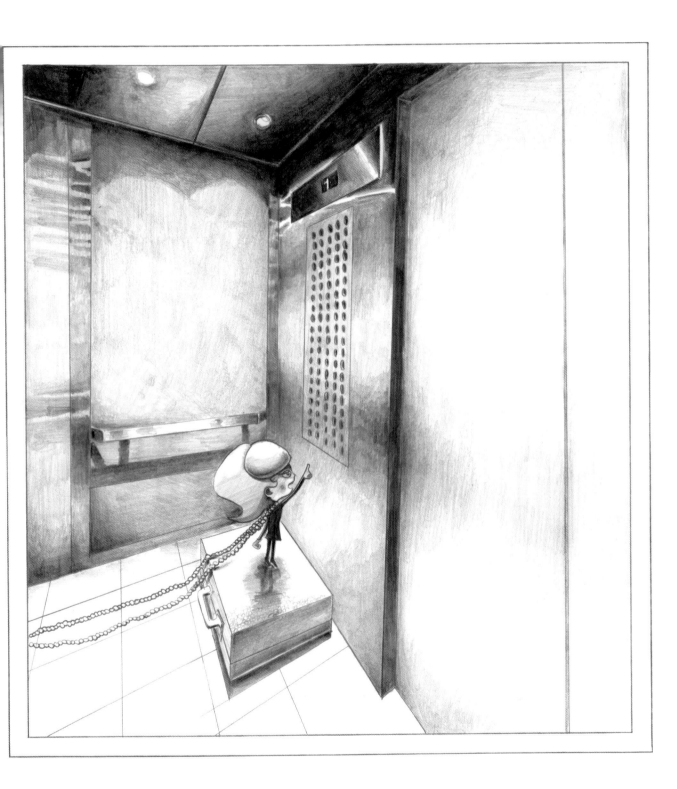

In the end, perhaps Isabel did what she was always meant to do.

I believe she would have called it her Last Power Breakfast.

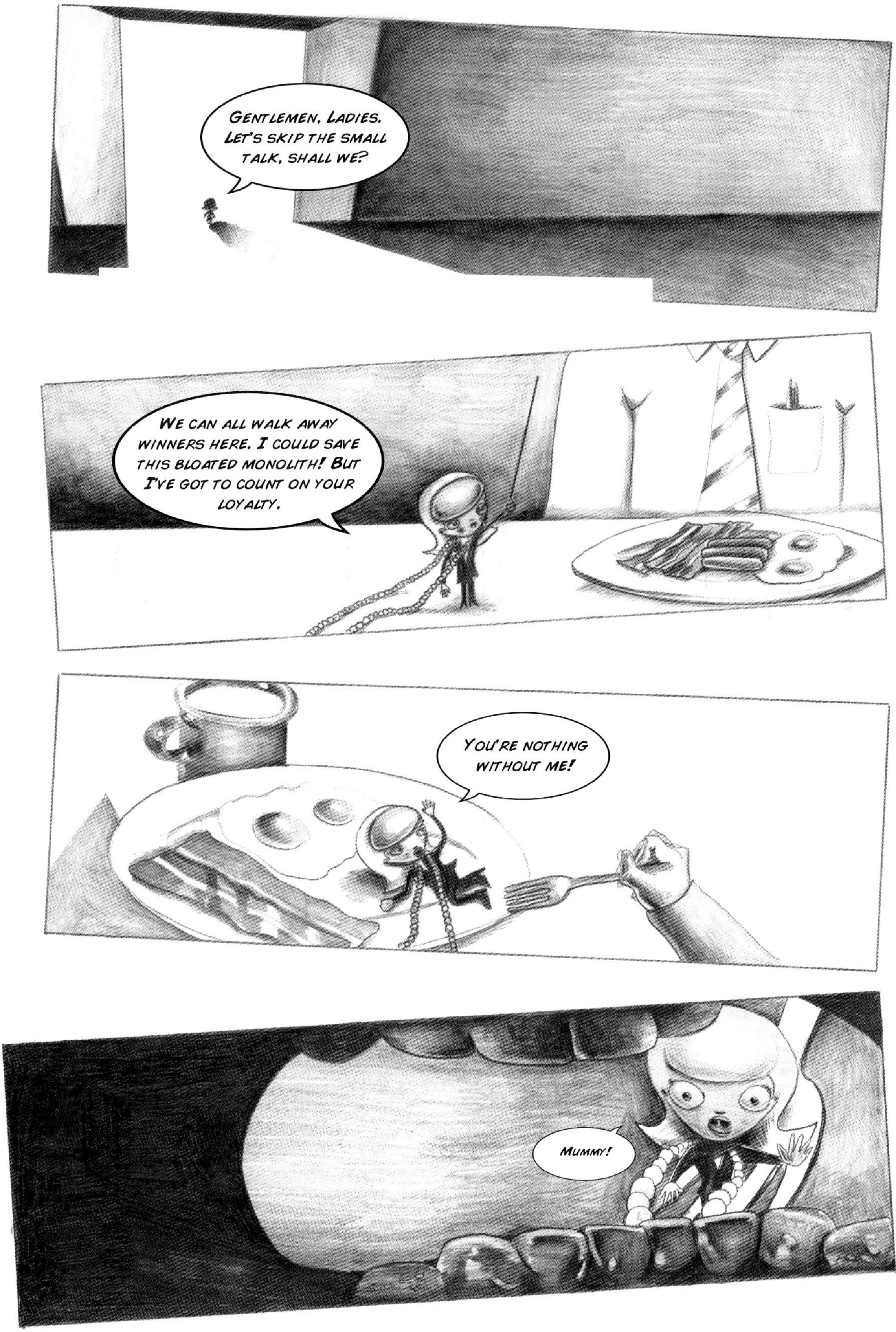
GENTLEMEN, LADIES. LET'S SKIP THE SMALL TALK, SHALL WE?
WE CAN ALL WALK AWAY WINNERS HERE. I COULD SAVE THIS BLOATED MONOLITH! BUT I'VE GOT TO COUNT ON YOUR LOYALTY.
YOU'RE NOTHING WITHOUT ME!
MUMMY!

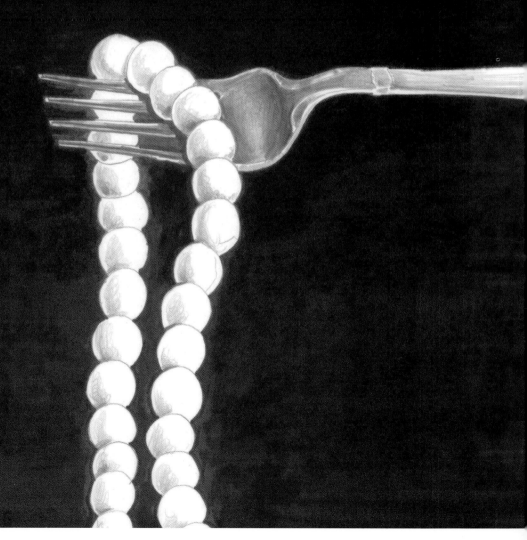

THE END ?

Not For Children CHILDREN'S BOOKS